Once Bitten, Twice Prepared

By Elaine Collier

Copyright 2021 by Elaine Collier
Cover by: Brown Creative
Designed by: Journey Written

Copyright 2021 Once Bitten, Twice Prepared all rights reserved. No part of this publication may be reproduced, stored in a retrial system, distributed, or transmitted in any form or by any means, including photocopying, recording, or other electric, or mechanical methods, without the prior written permission of the author, this also includes conveying via e-mail without permission in writing from the author.

ISBN 13: 978-1-7367389-0-0

Printed in the U.S.A

First Printing, 2021

Dedication

To Pat, thank you for being there through all the bad days and picking me up when I felt I couldn't go on – I love you

To Jordan, thank you for holding space for me, understanding me so completely and being my inspiration – I love you

To Gill, thank you for listening to me, crying with me and making me laugh – I love you

"One day you will tell your story of what you're going though, and it will become part of someone's survival guide."

~ Tiny Buddha

Once Bitten, Twice Prepared

Table of Contents

- v   Introduction
- 1   Section 1: Life Before Diagnosis
- 3   Section 2: Breast Cancer
- 27   Section 3: Life After Cancer
- 38   Section 4: Cancer the Second Time
- 70   Section 5: Spiritual Me
- 84   Section 6: My Survival Guide
- 100 Section 7: And Finally…

INTRODUCTION

Let me tell you a little about me. I am a spiritual being living in this world. But please don't think I'm floating about in the clouds somewhere sitting in the lotus position, burning incense and chanting. Oh no – I'm as down to earth as they come. I live in this world, and I love being here although it does get a bit shitty at times.

I live with my non-blood family, Pat, and Geoff, and a soppy cat called Roxy in Oxfordshire. We all get on well and together we are a support team. I first met Pat over 30 years ago when I changed my job. We got to know one another through our love of the social life where we worked. We quickly became good friends and spent a lot of time together along with our husbands, Denis and Geoff. When my life changed completely, both Pat and Geoff were there for me and gave me all the support and help I needed. Pat became everything I wanted all rolled into one person. We may not be connected by blood but we are family.

I have a son, Jordan, who is currently living in Bali with his lovely partner Adelya. I run the Como Centre, together with my best friend Gill, where we teach about all things mind, body and spirit. I have a love of life: I love people, I like to party, I like a drink (gin is good), oh, and I tend to swear a lot!

So, I'm now going to take you on a journey. My journey. It's been a major part of my life in that it affected me greatly at the time and I still live with the effects of it all. However, I will not let that journey define me.

I was first diagnosed with breast cancer in 2006 at the age of 52. Fast forward to fourteen years later and another breast cancer arrives in the same breast. My story is the difference between my two breast cancer journeys and how my spirituality and my personal development helped me cope with and deal with the second diagnosis in a much more positive way and brought about my own regime of how to push through when things go tits up.

Although my story is about cancer, it could equally have been about any other major issue that was affecting my life. I want you to see how I handled the two cancer diagnoses in two very different ways. I want to show you that there are things you can do, and techniques you can use, to help make your journey a little easier, whatever your journey is. This is not about finding a cure or a quick fix, it's about finding your way through in the best way possible for you.

Let's dive head first into my story. It's not the loveliest of tales but it's not all doom and gloom either.

LIFE BEFORE DIAGNOSIS

I had a lovely home in Oxfordshire where I lived with my non-blood family, Pat and Geoff, and a couple of cats. My son, Jordan, had finished university and was on a mission of self-discovery and traveling the world, so life was changing for me. It was time, maybe, to do something different for myself.

I worked full time as a PA to the Director of a Research Institute. I loved my job, and I loved the people I worked with. I am a real people person, I love talking and socializing. There's nothing I love more than a good night out with friends and a few drinks. We had a very active social club at the Institute and I was on the committee. My life was full-on with the full-time job, home life, and organizing social events, from quiz nights to summer balls, to shows and pantomimes. There was always something going on and I was usually slap bang in the middle of it.

We took some fabulous holidays and I loved traveling to new places. I particularly loved East Asia and loved seeing wildlife in its natural environment. One of my best holidays was in Borneo and getting up close to Orangutans. We always managed to meet great people on any holiday, and in Borneo, we met a lovely couple and spent a lot of time sightseeing with them and sharing great conversation and a few drinks in the bar during the evenings. I lived for my holidays and I thrived on the excitement from the moment we booked until the day we went.

We had a great group of friends who we often used to holiday within the Greek Islands. We would all get together at least once a month for dinner at one of our homes. In between, there would be trips to the cinema, a meal out, or just a few drinks down the pub. We laughed a lot, often uncontrollably, and life was good.

My life was full-on, enjoyable, and fun. Yes, we had a few problems crop up along the way as everyone does, but nothing we couldn't handle. I expected my life to continue in the same way well into old age.

I had a really good, happy, and contented life. I often wondered how I got to be so lucky.

BREAST CANCER

- DIAGNOSIS -

It was December 2005, and I was having my first ever mammogram at the age of 52. In the UK, we get a regular screening every 3-years after the age of 50. I had my mammogram in the mobile screening unit that comes to our local health centre. It was quick and easy, not painful but a little uncomfortable when your boobs get squashed between two metal plates. Nevertheless, it was done and that was that for another 3 years. They told me I would get the results in about 3 weeks. I went home and put the whole thing out of my mind. After all, Christmas was coming and Jordan, my son, was coming home for the holidays. I was beyond excited to see him again and with a houseful of people for Christmas, I had a lot to do.

A week later an envelope from the hospital popped through the door. I knew immediately what it was and knew it was not good news. That gut feeling – intuition – just kicked in. The envelope was too thick for one thing. It contained a lot of paperwork just to tell me I was all clear. It was also too early to be good news.

I felt a bit sick and I felt like I needed to run to the loo! Bad news of any kind always affects my stomach and I'd usually just have to sit on the loo and wait until my bowels empty completely. I knew I had to open the envelope but I really didn't want to. I wanted to run after the postman and hand it back to him.

Pat heard the post come through the letterbox so she came into the kitchen to see if there was anything for her. I showed her the letter. She asked me if I wanted her to open it, but to be honest, it didn't matter who opened it, the results were going to be the same. As I pulled the sheets of paper from the envelope, a map of the hospital fell to the floor and I knew then that I was being called in. Our hospitals in the UK are large complexes and most of them send maps out with appointments.

Pat stayed with me as I fumbled with the paperwork, she was as anxious as I was and probably just as scared. No, she couldn't have been as scared as me because her hair wasn't about to fall out. The letter said that the mammogram hadn't given a clear reading and they wanted me to have a scan. This time I had to go to the Churchill Hospital, which is our local cancer hospital in Oxford. I was given a date – the 19th of December, just before Christmas.

I was in pieces. This wasn't supposed to happen. It was all supposed to be ok. This was my first-ever mammogram; I wasn't old enough to have cancer. My world was falling apart. I cried - a lot. Things like this didn't happen to me. *Why is this happening?* I remember standing in the kitchen and I just knew on some level that I had cancer and that I would lose all my hair. I sobbed – I was more upset at that point about losing my hair, completely overlooking the fact that I might actually die! Pat held me as I cried, there was nothing she could say other than that she was there with me and that somehow, we would get through it.

I can't begin to explain those emotions, and they just kept coming, wave after wave. I couldn't switch them off and my head was full of all sorts of rubbish. There wasn't enough room in my head to think about anything other than cancer and what was going to happen. I couldn't seem to function on any other level. Mainly, I was seeing a bald-headed me. *What was it with losing my hair?* Surely there was more to worry about than my bloody hair, but that was my overriding thought. I very rarely went out of the house without makeup on, mainly because I looked like an extra from 'Day of the Dead' without it, so how on earth could I go out now, how could I go to work? I just knew that I wouldn't want to be seen by anyone.

I wanted to run away. Maybe if I went somewhere else I could leave all this cancer rubbish behind me. I just wanted to run, and run, and run. Bit like Forest Gump, if you've ever seen that film. One day he just started running and he ran for around 3-years. Oh, I wish I could run for 3-years, it would all be over by then. But I knew it didn't work like that and that I couldn't just bury my head in the sand. I had to deal with it, whatever it was and whatever it may bring, but I certainly didn't want to. I just wanted to run away.

- THE JOURNEY BEGINS -

December 19th, I remember the date well. Just a few days before Christmas, the day of my hospital appointment arrived. Oh, how I dreaded this. I felt sick, I needed the loo, I couldn't breathe properly. The drive to the hospital seemed to go on forever. Pat was with me and was talking a load of endless drivel trying to distract me. It didn't work and I think I told her to shut up in the end.

The waiting room was full of women who looked scared to death. Some of them would be ok and would be given good news, maybe I would be one of them. But what if I wasn't, how would I cope? Eventually, my name was called, and rather than the mammogram I was expecting, it was a scan.

As I walked into the room I saw a couch and the scanning machine. It was an ultrasound, much like they use on pregnant women to see the gorgeous and precious new life within. There was going to be nothing gorgeous and precious showing up for me! The nurse asked to remove my top and bra and lie on the couch, she covered me to preserve modesty. The woman doing the scan applied gel to my breast and then ran the hand-held scanner over the right side. She was going backwards and forwards, over and over again. Perhaps she couldn't find what she was looking for, I thought, perhaps there was nothing there at all. I am ever the optimist you see.

But no, she didn't like what she saw. I could see on the screen what she was looking at, a dark mass. She told me she didn't like the look of what she was seeing and wanted to do a biopsy. I wasn't expecting that either. I was scared, I didn't want it done. One, that it might hurt, but mainly because of what it might show. Memories of being a child at the dentist came back. I used to cry and beg to be allowed to go home and come back tomorrow. That's exactly how I felt in that room. But it had to be done.

They placed some numbing gel around the area and then a local anaesthetic was injected into the breast. That stung a bit! She went into the breast several times with some kind of instrument which pinched out bits of the mass. It didn't really hurt, just felt a bit uncomfortable. When it was all done and they told me that because of the Christmas break, the results wouldn't be back until the New Year and my next appointment would be sent to me through the post. This was not shaping up to be the Christmas I wanted it to be!

- CHRISTMAS -

Christmas in our house was always a hectic but joyous time. To be honest, I think I enjoyed the run-up to Christmas just as much, if not more than Christmas itself. There was always so much preparation to be done, with shopping, wrapping presents, cooking, cleaning, etc. When I was a kid my mum insisted that the house was cleaned from top to bottom otherwise Father Christmas wouldn't come. That stayed with me, so a thorough clean had to be done. I love this time: the smells of Christmas cooking, music playing, everyone happy. I love preparing for people, making sure everything is as perfect as it can be so they all have a good time.

This year Jordan was coming home and I was beyond excited. We were also having a houseful of people with family and friends all there. Nine of us for Christmas Day, how the hell was I going to keep smiling? I felt that my joy of Christmas was being stolen.

I did keep smiling though, and somehow, we got through Christmas Day. I didn't have the right to steal their joy at Christmas so I acted as if everything was normal. And it would have been absolutely normal if that sodding tumour hadn't decided to take up residence in my right breast. But putting on the 'everything is ok' act didn't stop the thoughts filling my head. Every now and then I caught myself wondering whether this would be my last Christmas, and I did sneak off for a little cry from time to time. I drank far more than I should have, just trying to block out reality.

But my worse day was still to come. If I thought December and Christmas was bad, 2nd January was the worse. Jordan left for more of his traveling adventures. This time, he was going to South America. I didn't want him to go but I didn't want him to stay either. I hadn't told anyone about the cancer. Well, to be honest, I hadn't had it confirmed by then so no point worrying everyone. Even if it was the worse, then there would be no point in him staying home, he wouldn't have been able to do anything. Best he went off to enjoy his adventures and have fun.

He left early in the morning. I got up to see him off but I just couldn't go to the airport. I never could do airport goodbyes, to be honest, just too painful for me. But when I hugged him goodbye that morning I really didn't know if that would be the last time I ever saw him. He went, full of joy and expectation of what was ahead, leaving behind me full of fear and dread of what was ahead.

I cried of course, he was used to me shedding a few tears every time he went away, but as soon as that car turned the corner and he was out of sight I just broke. I remember falling onto the hall floor and I sobbed in a way I never knew was possible, it really broke my heart. This was the worse time ever of having to say goodbye to my child. The ache in my heart was palpable. I had no idea how I would get through the next few days, let alone what was to come.

It seemed to take forever until I got the date for the next hospital appointment and the results of the scan. I had managed to get through Christmas and the New Year, and saying goodbye to Jordan, but the not knowing was turning me into an anxious nervous wreck. I became irritable and snapped at people. I was living in fear of what was ahead. I was my own worst enemy and was forever Googling breast cancer and frightening myself even more. The worse part of all of this was the waiting. Endless bloody waiting. So much time on my hands for my mind to come up with all sorts of worse case scenarios. By the end of that first week in January, I had convinced myself that my whole body was riddled with cancer.

Finally, the appointment came and I found myself back sitting in the hospital waiting room. The fear was suffocating. Again, I wanted to get up and run. Pat was with me, forever holding my hand and supporting me. I saw a lady doctor who didn't beat about the bush. She told me straight away that it was indeed cancer and that my next step would be surgery. An appointment would be made for me to see the surgeon as soon as possible. The results of the surgery would dictate the next steps to be taken.

And that was it. I had cancer. I wanted to know the end result. I wanted to know if I was going to die and what sort of treatment would I have to have. The doctor couldn't tell me any more at that point and suggested that I just take it one step at a time. Ha, easy for her to say, she wasn't the one going through it! And that was it! I remember crying in the hospital corridor, Pat trying to comfort me as best she could. Again, all I could think about was losing my hair. *How vain and trivial was that?* But it was my overriding thought and I've since come to understand that it's a common fear amongst a lot of women.

I came home and tried as best I could to live normally until the next appointment. I hadn't told anyone outside of the house about the cancer and it was like living with a great big secret, I was sitting on a time-bomb just waiting to go off! I did tell my boss at work. He and I had a good working relationship and he would quickly know that there was something not quite right, not to mention the time I needed to take off for hospital appointments. remember standing in his office first thing in the morning and I just blurted out: "I have breast cancer". He put his arms around me and let me cry, then told me it would all be ok, I could get through it, and that he would give me all the support I needed. I was not to worry about my job, just take all the time I needed. And so, we all settled down for the interminable wait for the next appointment.

I didn't know what type of surgery I was to have until I saw the surgeon. I didn't want to lose my breast so a mastectomy wasn't what I wanted. I knew I would have to do whatever it took to get rid of the cancer, but I just hoped it wouldn't be that radical. I was only 52 years old, I wasn't ready to lose parts of my body and especially what I still thought of as an important part of me. This waiting and imagining all sorts of things was hell. I understood the power of spiritual healing and visualisation from my time spent with the Spiritualist Church, so it was time to put it into practice.

I knew roughly where the tumour was although I couldn't feel it. Every night I went to bed I would call in an army of soldiers. In my mind, they looked like toy soldiers: black trousers and red tunics with a big busby type hat on their heads. They carried rifles, upright and tight against their bodies. They were fully equipped to deal with the enemy. My soldiers entered my body through my right foot and marched their way up to my right breast. There they formed a circle around the tumour, facing inwards. They stood to attention preventing the tumour or any cells escaping. They contained it in one place. I hoped that was enough to stop the cancer spreading until I could get the bloody thing removed from my body. It's a weird feeling to have something in your body that you know will kill you. I desperately wanted that tumour out and I wanted it out immediately. I needed to do something to help myself and calling in my army was the only thing I could think of that might just buy me some time.

Late January came about and it was time to meet my surgeon. Oh, I did not want to do this. I just wanted to run away, bury my head in the sand. But I had to just get on with it because I need to get this cancer out of my body. Once again, the waiting room was horrendous. Lots of frightened women in fear for their lives. Fear of the unknown.

My surgeon, Miss Clark, was a lovely woman. She discussed the results of the biopsy with me and offered me the choice of a mastectomy or a wide local incision (lumpectomy). She went on to say that at that time she felt there was no need to go for a mastectomy but that a lumpectomy to just remove the tumour and some lymph nodes would be adequate. I opted for the lumpectomy. I didn't want to lose my breast and the thought of being disfigured was just too much. She couldn't tell me what came after surgery until the results of the analysis of the removed tissue came back.

Surgery would be in about 3-weeks and the wait would make no difference to the tumour. The date for surgery would be posted to me. Nothing else to do other than go home and wait - again. Oh, the bloody waiting! It seems like forever that I've just been waiting. My whole life is just about waiting. *Will this thing never be over?* Again, I am plagued by thoughts of death. I could die on the operating table. At least that would be quick and I wouldn't lose my hair. My mind is just a bizarre mix of thoughts.

I only told my boss and a few people I worked closely with about the cancer. I decided to wait and see exactly what we were dealing with. I mean, I could have had the surgery and found out that it was nothing more than a cyst and then I could have just got on with my life, and no-one needed to know. I am basically an optimist and always try to find the brighter side of any situation. That does have a tendency to bite me on the arse though!

The day of surgery finally arrived and I had to be at the hospital early on the Monday morning. By now we're into February and at long last I felt that something positive was happening. I was very nervous but at the same time relieved to be getting rid of this thing residing in my right boob. I was around the middle of the list to go down to theatre so I had the whole morning to wait. I knew that when they removed the tumour they had to remove an area around it too to give clear margins. If the margins were unclear or the lymph nodes showed signs of cancer, then I would need further surgery. Bloody hell, I don't want to go through this again so I hope she gets the lot out in one go! Eventually, they came and got me and I was wheeled off. Nerves were really kicking in big time. My mouth had gone dry, I could hardly swallow let alone speak. The anaesthetist was having a bit of trouble finding a vein in my left arm but finally got the cannula in and asked me to count backwards. I don't remember anything beyond six. I woke up in recovery and the relief that flooded through me was enormous. It was over, done, that horrible bloody cancer had been removed from my body.

Back on the ward I was made comfortable, checked regularly and given pain relief. I wasn't in too much pain but certainly uncomfortable. I had two wounds, one for the tumour and one for the lymph node removal, with drains in each. The surgeon came around later in the day to tell me surgery had been successful. Although the tumour was bigger than expected, she was confident that it had been removed with clear margins and only three lymph nodes had been taken. I would be in hospital until the drains ran clear and the stitches could be removed, probably about 5-days.

My week in the hospital wasn't too bad at all. The women in the ward got on well and we all gathered together in the Common Room at the end of the ward to eat our meals, drink coffee, chat, etc. We could make our own tea and coffee when we wanted and were encouraged to be out of bed and fairly active. With my drains and stitches out, I was allowed home on the Friday. Recovery went smoothly and I was back to work within two weeks. I was really happy that the tumour had gone, and I felt really well.

- THE RESULTS -

Two weeks later, I had to go back to the hospital for the results. I still very nervous but the main thing was the cancer had gone. I met with some of the ladies I had been in hospital with, so we had a nice little chat which helped a little with the anxiety of waiting.

The tumour was a grade 3 triple negative. Apparently, that's quite aggressive. The good news was that they had clear margins and the lymph nodes were clear too, so the cancer hadn't spread. My team of soldiers I sent in during my self-healing had done a good job and contained the tumour. However, because of the type and grade of cancer, plus my age, I was to have chemotherapy followed by radiotherapy. An appointment would be made with the Oncologist and it would come through the post. I was beginning to dread the postman coming to our house.

I went home to wait again. But at least the tumour was gone and the cancer hadn't spread. Chemo was not what I wanted and I would definitely lose my hair. I Googled chemotherapy and bloody hell, it sounded horrendous. Pat assured me we could do this, yes it might be a bit tough for a while and yes, I would lose my hair, but we could do it. I've come to hate the term "we"! What is it with people who say 'we'? It's never going to be 'we', it's only ever going to be just 'me'. Yes, you may be there with me, witnessing my distress and trying to help as best you can, but it's only ever going to be 'me' going through it.

During the meeting with the Oncologist he gave me all the statistics of why I was to have chemotherapy. For a woman of my age, with my type of cancer, I had something like an 89% chance of still being alive after 5-years with both chemo- and radiotherapy treatments. Arrangements would be made to start the treatment and an appointment would be sent to me through the post. The Oncologist explained that although the tumour had been removed, there was a possibility that there may still be some cancerous cells flying around my body which are impossible to detect. The chemotherapy would mop up any stray cells anywhere in my body and the radiotherapy would target and kill any cells specifically in the breast area. Home to wait.

Strange emotions this time, here I was cancer-free now and feeling well. Life was getting back to normal, I was back at work and my social life was resuming. But I knew that in a few weeks that would all change again as chemo started. A cloud of doom hung over me. I planned to continue working throughout, although my boss told me to take all the time I needed. I was convinced that this was not going to affect me too much at all, that the worse was over.

I became impatient. I wanted to get on with this. For God's sake, why did everything take so long? The sooner I got on with this the quicker my hair would grow back!

Once surgery was done and I had the results I decided that it was probably time to tell people. I knew what I was facing and once my hair started to fall out they would know anyway. I told Jordan first by simply saying that I had surgery which went very well and the cancer had been removed. I said that I needed some follow-up treatment with chemotherapy and radiotherapy but that would fine and then it would be over. I told my Dad the same story. Neither of them knew how scared I was and even my friends and other family didn't have any idea about the emotions that were washing through me.

It was strange because at the beginning everyone was very kind and I received loads of well wishes, cards and flowers from family, friends, and colleagues. As time went on the messages started to dwindle and friends that I had for years seemed to keep their distance. One really good friend never ever contacted me although I knew that he knew I had cancer. I found this extremely hurtful, I couldn't understand why he couldn't even wish me well when I had been there for him during a dark period of his life. I understand that not everyone knows what to say in these situations, but surely he could have sent a short message to let me know he was thinking about me.

My life was on hold. I couldn't make plans or book a holiday because I simply didn't know what was going to happen next. I had so many hospital appointments stacking up that there really wasn't time to do much else. My whole life revolved around the hospital, the doctor's surgery, appointments, treatments, and bloody cancer.

- CHEMOTHERAPY -

Mid-March and my first day of chemo arrived. I'd had all the necessary blood tests to make sure it was ok to go ahead, and taken all the right medication, and there I was sitting in the chemo suite. Eventually, they got a cannula into my left arm and the chemo infusion began. I was surrounded by people sitting in those big blue hospital chairs and in various stages of illness. I didn't like it one bit, was that how I would soon look? There was I with my make-up on and hair done to be faced by the harsh realities of what was to come.

To say chemo and I didn't get on was a bit of an understatement. I had probably one of the worse possible times of my life getting through that treatment. But I should add here that it's not the same for everyone. We are all different and tolerate the drugs and procedures differently. You don't know at the start how you will react, but please don't let my experience of chemotherapy put you off getting treatment that could possibly save your life. I explain my experience here only to show you why I later made the choices I did.

Chemo number one went fairly well once they got a cannula into my vein. The chemo seemed to flow through my body quickly and when I nipped to the loo before coming home my pee had already turned bright pink. I felt fine though and drove myself home. Feeling fine lasted until the evening and then the vomiting started. It went on for 3-days and I felt so ill. I couldn't eat, water tasted foul and the bloody anti-sickness pills were not doing their job. I stank of chemicals. There was no way I was doing this again, I never wanted to feel like this again, I'll just take my chances and die if I must.

I phoned the chemo suite for advice and was told to increase the dose. They always started on the lowest dose to see how patients went, but doubling the dose should do the trick. Bloody hell, three days of throwing up and I could have just doubled the dose! I soon started to feel better, started to eat again and even went back to work.

- THE HAIR ISSUE -

Two milestones were reached during this feeling well phase – I got my wig and had my head shaved.

I went with Pat and a friend I had made in the hospital during surgery to get my wig. Funny thing was she turned out to be the mum of one of Jordan's friends and only lived a couple of villages away. At that time, chemo patients were given a voucher towards the cost of the wig. It was enough to buy a cheap one or you could pay the difference if you wanted something better. I thought I would go for a complete change and try long hair. I had always kept my hair short as it was much easier to manage, so this was a good opportunity to try something completely different. On went the long wig and I looked awful. I tried blond, brunette, red, and even some of the blues and pinks. I tried curly and straight, but nothing looked right and I just looked like a parody of me. I ended up with a wig that matched my own style and colour, so no dramatic change for me.

It was such a fun-filled morning trying on different wigs and laughing at some dramatic and ridiculous changes. We both got our wigs and then went out to lunch to celebrate the wig and completing our first chemo cycle. A good day in a gloomy time.

A week or two after my first treatment I noticed that my hair was starting to thin, so I took the bull by the horns and asked my hairdresser to shave my head. My hair was short anyway, but I just couldn't bear the thought of finding clumps of it on the pillow or flowing down the drain when I had a shower. If I had to lose my hair, and it seems I did, then I wanted to be in control of it. God knows I was in control of little else right now so I would choose when to lose my hair. My hairdresser was a gem and came to the house. She shaved it really short, but not completely off. It gave me time to get used to the new me with a new shape head. Friends told me it looked good. But that was now, wait until I was a complete slap head!

Those good days were few and far between so when they did show up I really made the most of them. I even went back to work.

- CHEMO NUMBER TWO -

I was back in the Chemo Suite and a real problem getting the cannula in a vein. I had to sit for half an hour with a heated blanket around my arm to try and bring the veins up. Eventually, it worked and the infusion done. This time I wasn't sick, but I felt nauseous for most of the time. My brain didn't seem to want to function, I couldn't think straight and it was as much as I could do to string a sentence together. It was like sinking into a deep, dark pit. It was scary and I had no way of knowing when, or even if, I would get out of that pit. I couldn't eat or drink, everything tasted foul and my body stank of chemicals, no matter how often I showered. The steroids turned me into a hyperactive zombie the minute I went to bed and I couldn't sleep. It took me about 3-days before I started to climb out of the pit. I tried every day to complete a Sudoku puzzle and the day I completed it was the day I knew I was crawling out.

This time the mouth ulcers started and heartburn like I've never had before seared its way down to my stomach. I went to my GP for something to help and it did provide some relief.

After about a week or so I went back to work. I wore the wig and was complemented on my new hairstyle. The wig was ok, but it was tight and made my head sweat. As soon as I got home I took it off in favour of a soft beanie type hat. My hair was really beginning to fall out now and my hair follicles hurt. I slept in the hat too as my head got cold at night. Two sessions down, four to go.

- CHEMO NUMBER THREE -

Getting into a vein proved impossible. It was decided that a PICC line needed to be inserted into my upper arm which would stay in place until all treatment was finished. I had a long wait until the specialist nurses came, but try as they might they could not get the line in. It would have to be a Hickman line into the neck and then out through the chest wall. Oh no, please, surely not. The wimp in me was coming out big time. Would they notice if I just went home? The nurses reassured me that I wouldn't feel a thing and I would be sedated. They suggested that Pat went and got a cup of tea because she really wouldn't want to watch this. For God's sake, this was about to get horrendous.

The next thing I remember was hearing Pat's voice as her head popped round the curtain of my bed, and the nurse telling her it was all done. I have no idea what they gave me but it was bloody good stuff and I never felt a thing. I felt like I had been out drinking but without the hangover. Within half an hour the chemo nurse started my infusion directly into the line and I left the hospital by about 7 pm that evening. It was a long day and I felt drained, but I was happy that the line was in and I wouldn't have to worry about finding a vein again.

The next day I slipped down into the pit. In vain I tried completing Sudoku's to try and bring myself out much quicker, but to no avail. Day 3 and I started to emerge. Then the mouth ulcers started and to make matters worse, I erupted at the other end with haemorrhoids! I went to my GP and she gave me some suppositories and cream, but they made little difference. It was painful and I started to take painkillers, which helped a bit.

After about a week I developed a temperature – an infection had set somewhere. I phoned the hospital and they wanted me in straight away. They needed blood and it should have been easy to just get it out of the Hickman line. No, nothing came out and nothing went in either. They had to find a vein! I was sent for an x-ray to see what the problem with the Hickman Line was. Seems like the line had twisted and was lying flat again the vein wall, hence nothing in and nothing out. The blood results back and my white blood cells were zero. I was neutropenic and yes, I had an infection. A cannula had to go in somewhere so I could be given antibiotics intravenously. I was becoming quite phobic every time anyone mentioned taking blood or getting a cannula in. I was in the hospital for 3-days.

I tried to go back to work but I wasn't feeling great. My bum hurt like hell and getting comfortable in the car was proving impossible. I remember that during that particular morning's drive I was thinking about death a lot and I eventually concluded that I would indeed have to die at some point, as we all did, but the upside was that I would only have to do it once! For some strange reason that cheered me up. Dying wouldn't be like chemotherapy where I would have to do it over and over again, it was a one-time-only job.

After I had been driving for about 20-minutes, the pain in my backside was becoming unbearable and I knew that sitting all day in the office was probably not a good idea. I turned the car around and went back home. I didn't go back to work after that. During the time Jordan was travelling we kept in touch by e-mail. He was travelling around a lot so his messages were intermittent. He didn't have a mobile phone with him, so he was reliant upon internet cafes, and Skype was not really an option. He knew by this time that I had surgery and was going through chemo, but I never told him just how bad it was. A couple of his friends were going out to join him for a while and Jordan asked one of them to pick something up from home to take out with him. His friend, Matthew, came to the house one day to collect the item and I could see the shock on his face when he saw me. I asked him not to tell Jordan how bad I looked, to just tell him I was fine. I can only presume he did because Jordan never said anything in his messages to me.

By now I was halfway through treatment with three sessions down, three to go.

- CHEMO NUMBER FOUR -

Chemo number 4 followed the same pattern as before. In addition, the piles were horrendously painful and bleeding. I dreaded having to go to the loo in the morning and I was living on painkillers although they were pretty ineffective. My energy levels were depleting. It was all I could do to get out of bed in the morning and take a shower. After showering I had to lie down for 20-minutes or so before I could get myself dressed. I spent my days lying on the sofa either reading or watching TV. I was taking stronger painkillers for the haemorrhoids and by lunch time I was getting a little relief as long as I kept lying down. This was no way to live was it, lying down all day with an excruciating pain in the arse!!

About a week later and the temperature shot back up, which meant I had to go back to the hospital. I still had the Hickman Line in although it wasn't working at all. Not quite sure why they didn't take it out, but at that point, I didn't really care. Eventually blood was taken. Not only did I have an infection, I was also badly anaemic and they needed to do a blood transfusion. However, I was losing a fair amount of blood from my bleeding piles so they sent me to another hospital to be examined. I went into Surgical Emergencies and the doctor I saw said it was an anal fissure and not just piles, so no wonder I was in a lot of pain. He said he needed to inject Botox into the fissure which would stop the bleeding and relieve the pain, but warned me that it wouldn't be high on my list of good things to do that day. My God, he was so right. The pain was absolutely excruciating. Pat was with me the whole time and I squeezed her hand so hard and begged her to make him stop. I'm sure I must have been screaming. I know I was certainly crying. I don't think I had ever had such a painful procedure – if that's Botox then you can keep it. Eventually, it was over I went back to the Churchill Hospital and settled into bed. The nurses laughed when they knew what had happened and said that I must have the smoothest arse in the hospital.

Next came a cannula. Oh, for fucks sake, was there no end to this day? The trouble was that because of the surgery on my right side, everything needed to either go in or come out of my left arm. Leaving a cannula and line in place would help but as my veins were beginning to close, it was becoming increasingly difficult. Eventually, they got a line in and the blood transfusion was set up to run overnight. As before I was neutropenic and had an infection, and on top of that, I was anaemic too.

Another 4-days in hospital. Four sessions down, only two to go. Emotionally, I was still all over the place and I felt so alone. I was certain that I was the only woman in the world going through what I was going through right now and trying to cope with how I really felt. I know I had Pat, and she was a God send and I don't know what I would have done without her, but she doesn't talk about emotions too easily. I was trying to stay strong and in control so as not to worry and upset my family, when all I wanted was to collapse in someone's arms and tell them how I really felt. I know my cancer was affecting her too and it would have been good if we could have both opened up fully, and told each other exactly how we were feeling.

- CHEMO NUMBER FIVE -

They decided to remove the Hickman Line. I wanted it out, but would it be as bad as getting it in? I was assured that getting it out was easy and I didn't even need a local anaesthetic. Really? Did they realise what a wimp I was? They were true to their word, however. It came out easily and all I felt was a little wriggling inside my chest. I was greatly relieved. Now, to get a cannula in. It was difficult as usual, but eventually the nurse found a suitable vein in the back of my arm. The infusion was given but just towards the end the vein gave up and the chemical started leaking directly into my arm just under the skin. It hurt and was burning. The nurse removed the cannula immediately but a lump had already started to form! God, I hope it would be ok. All I needed now was my arm to turn black and drop off.

Chemo took the same pattern as before but at least my bum was better! A week in and my temperature shot up, but by this time, I really didn't care. was so weak and felt so ill, I wanted everyone to leave me alone so I could just die. I felt I was rotting from the inside out. But Pat was having none of it and got me to the hospital. She had to find a wheelchair to get me to the ward, I couldn't even walk. I was shivering despite it being June and warm temperatures. I can't remember ever feeling so ill, please just let me die.

By now my veins had just about given up so a doctor was called, and after much prodding and poking, and stabbing me with umpteen million needles, he managed to get one in my foot. Bloods taken and the wait for results began, but I knew what it would be.

I had depleted white blood cells and infection so I had to go back on antibiotics. By this stage, I really didn't care what they pumped me full of. I felt awful, exhausted, and just wanted it to be all over. I had had enough. This time the antibiotics caused diarrhoea and getting to the bathroom seemed like a marathon, especially pushing the drip trolley that was feeding into my left foot. The nurses took pity on me a brought me a commode to use but oh, how I hated that. What on earth was all this coming to? I couldn't even deal with my own personal hygiene now. I couldn't live like this, but maybe I wouldn't have to for much longer. This was surely the end of the road for me and, to be honest, I didn't care.

Two days later, a big black boil thing appeared under my right arm, where I had surgery. Oh my God, look at me. Would I end up with black pustules all over my body? Maybe I had bubonic plague. A nurse came around and told not to worry but they needed to test me for MRSA, but if it was positive there were treatments I could be given. My stepmother died when she caught MRSA in hospital so I wasn't too confident. But I really didn't care, please just let me die.

Day three and my body started to respond to the antibiotics. My white cell count was coming back up and I was beginning to fight back. By day four, I was feeling much better, maybe there was hope for me after all. Day five and they were making noises about discharging me, but first, another blood test and a chat with my oncologist. The blood test showed that my platelets were depleted so I needed an infusion. The oncologist came and asked how I was feeling and I told him immediately that I didn't think I could do this anymore and, much to my surprise, he agreed with me.

I cannot begin to tell you how relieved I was, I cried. In fact, I sobbed. I cried a lot that day but they were tears of pure relief and joy. He said that the chemotherapy was taking my body down more each time and as I had already completed five cycles he saw no valid reason to put me through the last one. I phoned Pat and sobbed down the phone. She couldn't understand a word I was saying and thought it was bad news. In the end, the nurse had to tell her what was happening. I cried on and off for most of that day. It was looking more and more likely that I would live and I would never have to go through the horrors of chemotherapy again.

Still relieved, I still had to wait for the platelets infusion, but was allowed home the following day, after another blood test of course. The platelets are a component of the blood and need to be at a certain level for blood clotting. With all the chemotherapy and antibiotic drugs, my platelets had taken a big dip and they needed to be topped up. Of course, this meant another cannula had to go in but by now I was becoming a total pin cushion. They decided to stop messing about and just go into the right arm, after all this was to be the last time they would hopefully need to get in. Cannula in, platelets delivered and bloods taken the following morning.

The results came back and the platelet count had gone back up. I could go home. I was euphoric! If this is what being on a drug-induced high was like then I could understand the attraction. Nothing could dampen my spirits, not even the migraine that started on the way home. I felt like a great weight had been lifted from me, I no longer had to suffer the horrors of chemotherapy and all the illness that it triggered in me. But of course, I couldn't remain in this high forever and slowly I came back down to earth. Again, I must say here that not everyone reacts in the same way to chemo. I was extreme and I don't know anyone else who reacted that badly. If you need chemotherapy then please go ahead and have it, because it may be the one thing that saves your life.

Once I got home I began to recover my strength and energy levels, albeit slowly. I started to eat again and Pat made sure I had a good variety of nutritious and healthy food. I still rested a lot but my interest in the tv, reading, and doing jigsaws started to return. It was World Cup year too so I watched a lot of football (or soccer). I was much happier and no longer wanted to die. But I still had to get through radiotherapy.

- GOOD THINGS BEGAN TO HAPPEN -

A few good things happened during the wait for my next lot of treatment. Some good friends popped by unexpectedly one day to see how I was doing now that chemo had finished. I still looked pretty grim, bald as a coot and still with that waxy chemo pallor, but I was feeling much better in myself. We sat and chatted for ages and then they asked if I felt up to going out for lunch. Did I ever! I hadn't been out of the house other than for hospital appointments for months so doing something social, fun and with good friends was exactly what I needed. We went to a lovely pub by the river, just outside of Oxford. It was a glorious July summer day and we found a table in the shade outside. I can't remember what I ordered to eat but I know it tasted wonderful. I also had my first glass of wine for many months. I just felt so alive, and so very happy to be alive, basking in that warm sunshine with friends who made me laugh. Oh, how I hoped there would be many more moments like that.

The next enjoyable event was held at the Maggie's Centre, a support centre for all types of cancer. Women going through chemotherapy can attend, totally free of charge, one of their Look Good, Feel Better sessions. You can choose when you want to attend, either at the beginning of chemo, halfway through or at the end. During these sessions, they have a team of beauty therapists come in, complete with a wide range of cosmetics, to show you how to apply make-up to a waxy face that is devoid of eyebrows and eyelashes in a way that makes you look really good. I had dabbled with applying makeup, but to be honest, I looked like a pantomime dame by the time I had finished. I opted to go to the session once I had finished all of my chemo treatments so I could really appreciate the experience without feeling ill. Numbers were limited to around 10 people and the weather was quite warm the day I attended. A lovely bubbly lady came in last and took the seat next to me. "Phew," she exclaimed, "it's bloody hot in here," and promptly pulled her wig off her head. Everyone stared wide-eyed but I just loved it. Here was someone being completely herself and not conforming to what others thought she should be. "Yes, it is," I said, and pulled my head covering off too. We both sat there as bald as coots and started to laugh, and then everyone else joined in. The ice was broken, we all laughed a lot and had a wonderful morning. I went home with my face made up beautifully and a bag full of cosmetics.

But the major thing that happened around that time was my hair started to grow back. I remember sitting in front of the mirror in the bedroom one morning and I saw a little bit of fuzz on top of my head. I couldn't believe it. I shouted for Pat. She thought something bad had happened as she rushed up the stairs. She couldn't see it a first. She felt my head and said that I was imagining it, but then the sunlight streaming in from the window caught it, and there it was. Fluff. I was overjoyed. I had lived with the thought of what if my hair never grew back? Could that happen? Would I be bald for the rest of my life? But here it was, the very start of hair.

- RADIOTHERAPY -

Eventually radiotherapy had to start and an appointment was made in early July for me to go and have the coordinates programmed into the machine. The machine needed to be calibrated with the exact coordinates for each individual patient and tiny pin-prick tattoos were placed in three different positions around my right boob. It took a while to get the machine set and I had to lie still for the entire time

time. It wasn't comfortable! I was given a top that was front opening and held together with Velcro. I had to wear it to each treatment so that the right boob could be exposed for treatment. It wasn't a pretty top and I hated it, but it was mine for the duration. I was also given my schedule of appointments, alternating between two one week then three the next for a total of about 6-weeks. I was told that I could expect to feel tired, which would increase as the weeks went on, and that there would possibly be skin breakdown around the area treated. Oh, what joys! Just as I had got over one lot of treatment, another lot started. I was hopeful though, that I wouldn't feel quite so ill as I did with chemotherapy, and that it wouldn't try to kill me. At least now I could see light at the end of the tunnel and in just six weeks, treatment would be over. Because of the type of tumour - triple negative - I didn't have to take any follow-on medication.

My first radiotherapy day dawned and off I went to the hospital, resplendent in the bloody awful top. I had no idea what to expect and so fear of the unknown kicked in. One good thing was that they didn't need to get a cannula in a vein. Thank heavens for small mercies. I waited a while and then I was called in. As I settled onto the table, a nurse placed my arms in the correct position and whipped open the Velcro on the top. She told me to lie still and then left the room. The machine moved into position, whirring, and humming and pumping radiation into my body but I didn't feel a thing. It was all over quite quickly and off I went home.

And so, the pattern continued for around 15 sessions. Some days I got in quickly, other days I had a long wait, especially when one of the machines broke down and everyone was queuing for the remaining one. The weeks went by. It was a bit of a faff having to drive to the hospital 2- and 3-times a week, especially when the traffic was bad, but slowly we got through it.

The treatment was nowhere near as bad as I expected. I'd heard all sorts of horrible things from women who'd had radiotherapy, but it seemed to me that if you had chemotherapy first then this treatment was more of a doddle. It was certainly a breeze for me.

Yes, I got tired but I came home and rested for a while. I didn't experience any skin breakdown. It got a bit pink towards the end but I slathered cream around the area as I was told to and that really did make a difference. My final day of treatment was sometime towards the end of August and I delighted in giving back the oh-so fashionably gross top, and I walked out of that hospital elated that I had completed all treatment. Yes, I still had to have check-ups but the harsh regime of treatments was over at long last.

Oh, what a rollercoaster ride that all was, and it went on for months. I hate rollercoasters, they can make me feel sick just looking at them. But I certainly took that ride whether I wanted to or not. I stepped on board when I went for the first mammogram, I was strapped into place and once someone pressed the start button I had no way of getting off. I was slowly taken up to dizzying heights where I thought it was all ok and moving nice and slowly, only to be dropped at breakneck speed and plunged into the depths of despair. It happened time and time again and in spite of my screaming: stop, I want to get off! Nobody heard me. I got on that ride feeling fit and well and enjoying life, but before long I was left feeling nauseous, vomiting, and so ill that I wanted to die.

LIFE AFTER CANCER

It was the strangest of feelings once treatment had finished. Yes, I still had to go back to the hospital for regular check-ups, but that long grueling slog of treatment was finally done. On the one hand, I was elated, I had done it and now I could get back to normal life. On the other hand, I was scared that there was no one to keep a close check on me. My next hospital appointment was 3-months away. Anything could happen in that time.

From day one of diagnosis, you enter the system, and the system takes over. You are told when to go to the hospital, when you will have this treatment, when you will have a blood test, when you will have medication, etc. Your life is mapped out for you and, to be honest, I just felt like a number. Those of you lovely readers of a certain age might remember the 60s TV show, The Prisoner. The main character was constantly told he was not a name but a number, and that's how I felt. I felt that no one really listened to me or took my thoughts and feelings into account, they had a job to do and my role was just to comply. I knew they only wanted to get me well again but when you're living in a highly emotional state most of the time, it's the little things like someone really listening to you matters and makes a big difference.

There's a big lack of emotional support within the hospital system. That is not a complaint and I totally understand why that is, but it would have made a huge difference if that support had been available at the time of an appointment when it's possibly needed the most. What I really wanted was someone to give me a hug and say: "I know exactly how you are feeling because I have been there too". We are very lucky because we have a Maggie's Centre at the hospital, which provides both practical and emotional support for all types of cancer. I've used them once or twice but to be honest I just wanted to get away from the hospital environment as quickly as possible.

One thing I did start to learn slowly was that I was never going to get back to the old me, the me that lived a fairly carefree life with not too much to worry about. Although I was in my 50s, I still had the immortal mentality, that nothing bad was going to happen to me and I was going to live forever. Bad stuff existed, yes, but that happened to other people and not me. Having cancer destroyed all that. I realised that I was as vulnerable as the next person. The cancer might come back and kill me next time. This whole scary episode had brought me kicking and screaming into the real world, it brought an element of fear with it and I had to learn to accept and live with the new me.

My hair was continuing to grow and what started as baby fluff was beginning to thicken. There were areas where it was thicker than others, but nevertheless, I had hair. My fear of being bald for the rest of my life was beginning to dwindle.

It was August Bank Holiday, the last public holiday in the UK before Christmas. It's a lovely long weekend to look forward to. My Dad came to stay with us, which was lovely as I hadn't seen him since the previous Christmas. I was looking forward to spending time with him and I know he wanted to see me and see for himself that I was really okay now. It was a gorgeous weekend, the weather was dry, sunny, and hot, which is rare for a bank holiday in this country. We were invited to spend the Monday with friends, enjoying their village fete in the afternoon and then a meal and evening at their home. Again, I was really looking forward to this because I knew we would all have a really good time with plenty of laughing - just what I needed. It was a scorching hot day and I was wearing a summer dress, but my head was sweating underneath the scarf that I was still wearing every time I went out. Eventually, I'd had enough and pulled the scarf off my head. My hair was still exceedingly short and I drew some stares from people, but my family and friends gathered round and said I looked amazing and congratulated me for ditching the scarf. I never wore it again after that.

When I got home I threw all the scarves in the bin and I put the wig up for sale on e-Bay. The wig actually sold for more than I paid for it. Another goodbye to cancer.

My hair continued to grow and thicken. The more it grew the curlier it became and I really loved it. My hair is naturally as straight as a die and having curls was a real novelty. Lovely soft loose curls all over my head. The only down-side was that they were grey. I didn't keep those curls for long however, the first time I had my hair cut the curls went and my hair returned to normal. The other odd thing that happened was all my fingernails started to fall out. I was sure it was a result of chemotherapy, but one by one they turned a funny colour, lifted, and dropped off. Underneath was a new nail, already formed and growing.

I went back to work at the beginning of September. It was a gradual phase back, starting with a couple of mornings a week. I must admit that the first couple of weeks were tiring and I came home exhausted. I think that as well as physically tiring I was feeling mentally drained too. I was not used to thinking and problem solving so much. But I slowly increased my hours and was back to working full time within a month. Life really was beginning to get back to normal.

At the beginning of October Jordan came home. I was beyond excited, I hadn't seen my boy for nearly a year. I cleaned his bedroom from top to bottom, fresh sheets on the bed and everything looking lovely for him. I knew it wouldn't last for 5-minutes once he got home, but that was not the point. Not only did I do his bedroom, I bought all his favorite foods too. I had missed him so much and loved him beyond reason, I wanted to spoil him rotten for a while. This was definitely an airport trip, so Geoff, Pat, and I set off for

Heathrow. For some strange reason, I was jittery and then the thoughts started – what if he'd missed the flight, what if he'd been stopped for some reason at the airport, what if he'd decided not to come home? On and on they went! I was constantly watching the arrivals board and at last there it was, his flight had landed. I rushed to get the best spot by the arrivals barrier and there I waited. It was taking forever, I knew he had to collect his baggage but even so. The thoughts started again: what if, what if, what if... and then the doors opened and there he was. He saw me and rushed over to the barrier and we had the biggest and longest hug we'd ever had. Of course, I cried, but this time they were tears of pure joy – I had my boy home.

He told me sometime later that he was actually shocked by my appearance. Although I thought I looked pretty good in comparison to what my appearance had been, my hair was still very short and I still had a slight look of having recovered from an illness.

- LIVING WITH THE SIDE EFFECTS -

It is a great feeling when all treatment is finished. It was especially nice for me as I didn't have to take any further medication. It's not the same for women who, after completing chemotherapy and radiotherapy, have to go on to take various drugs for the next 5-years or so. What nobody ever really tells you is the consequences and side effects of all the treatments, some of which remain for the rest of your life. I certainly suffered the after effects of both my treatments and still do to this day.

Later in October, we decided to take a long weekend trip to Belgium. We went on Eurostar to Brussels and although the weather was lousy, it was so lovely to get away and do something completely different. We had a good hotel in the centre of the city so within easy reach of public transport and easily found our way around. One night we were having dinner in a lovely restaurant and suddenly I started to experience pins and needles down one side of my face and over my face and over my head. It lasted for about 20-minutes and then faded away. I didn't say anything to the others at the time, and I really didn't think too much of it. But then it happened a couple more times over that weekend. It was beginning to worry me.

The tingling continued after we got back home and eventually I went to the doctors. He wasn't sure what it was, but as I had just had breast cancer, he felt we should get it checked out. He sent me off to the hospital for a brain scan. I was beside myself with fear and convinced that it was a brain tumour. How on earth was I going to survive this? It was one thing to have breast cancer, you could have your boob lopped off if necessary. But a brain tumour was a whole new ball game. You couldn't have your brain removed! I had the scan and then saw a consultant. She was very nice, asked me loads of questions, and told me to try not to worry. The results would take a week or so and then we would have another chat. Try not to worry my arse, I was consumed by worry. Three days later and she phoned me at work. That scared me, it had only been a few days and I wasn't expecting a phone call. But she called to say she thought I would like to know as soon as possible that the scan was clear – I didn't have a brain tumour. She went on to say that she thought the tingling could be a form of migraine presenting in a different way. I didn't think for a minute that it was a migraine but I was greatly relieved that I didn't have a brain tumour.

For the past year, my life seemed to be one gigantic rollercoaster. I was either in the depths of despair with a body riddled with cancer, or I was like some drug fuelled junkie euphoric on relief and joy. All I wanted was a bit of stability for a while, for my life to be on an even keel with nothing to worry about. Was I asking for too much?

About a month after my chemotherapy treatments finished, the mouth ulcers started. I was plagued with them and mainly down the sides of my tongue. Why was I getting them now? I had them a lot during treatment but, surely, they should have stopped now. It seemed as soon as one cleared up I would get a few days of respite and then another would erupt. They were so painful. I bought tube after tube of various ointments and lotions to dab on them, which helped for a while and then the pain would start again. This went on for a while and I went to the doctors. She could find no reason and gave me a prescription for more of the ointments and lotions. I went to the dentist who of course mentioned oral cancer, although he was quick to add that in his opinion this was not cancer. If it was cancer then the ulcers would not heal, mine were healing well in between eruptions. But never mind the reassurance, he'd planted the seed! For the next 5-years I lived with these recurring mouth ulcers. During the painful eruptions, I convinced myself that it was oral cancer and that I would have to have half my face removed! Oh, the mind is a dangerous thing.

Eventually, my dentist retired and my replacement was a much younger lady who I really liked. I told her about the ulcers and she could see the scarring they had left on the tongue. She said she didn't think it was cancer at all, and said that there could be one or two other conditions that could be causing the problem and it could actually be a consequence of chemotherapy. This was music to my ears because every time I brought up the subject with the old dentist and even my GP, I was told categorically no that was not the case. My new dentist wanted to refer me to the hospital for a specialist opinion. Oh God, here we go again! After another long wait, I finally got the appointment. I was trying to remain calm and sensible but the mind was kicking in big time. By the time I got my appointment, I had just about convinced myself that it was indeed cancer and that I would probably need my head chopped off!!

The consultant questioned me, looked in my mouth, even took photos and finally said that it wasn't cancer. He thought I had a condition called Oral Lichen Planus which was an autoimmune condition and could well have been triggered by chemotherapy! He wanted to keep an eye on it, just to see if or how it worsened so I went back several times. It didn't get any worse and in fact it started to improve. I had longer periods of time between eruptions and I was feeling so much better about the whole thing. On my final hospital visit, the consultant told me that he thought stress could be my trigger and looking back I could see where he was coming from with that. I'd had so much stress over recent years, a lot of which was blown out of all proportion by myself, so it's no wonder my body reacted in some way.

What pleased me more than anything was that someone had actually said that it could have been as a result of chemotherapy. For too long I had lived with the medics denying that chemotherapy had such side effects, and side effects that I and many other women would have to live with for the rest of our lives. Knowing this didn't prevent flare-ups of the mouth ulcers, but it did put my mind at rest that my head wouldn't have to be amputated!

Slowly life was beginning to get back to some sort of normal. It wasn't like before, I wasn't that same carefree type of person I was before. Yes, I was totally delighted that I had made it through and was cancer-free, but I constantly had a cloud of fear over my head – what if it came back? I don't think anyone who has been through a major illness or event in their lives can be the person they were before it happened. It doesn't mean the new you is worse than before, it can often be better, but you are certainly different.

Life was good. I was back at work and my social life was picking up again. I was still having regular check-ups at the hospital and they were all good. Fear and anxiety still crept in before each appointment, the "what ifs" started. I remember one time: it was my first annual mammogram after treatment finished. The mammogram had been done and I thought that was it, I could go home and my results would be sent through the post. But no, I was told to go and sit back in the waiting area and the doctor would see me shortly. No, that wasn't right! That's not the way it's supposed to happen. That's it, it's back, they've seen it on the screen – another bloody tumour! Pat was with me that morning but as soon as I told her I had to wait as the doctor wanted to see me, she rushed off to the loo. As she was losing the contents of her bowel down the toilet, I was literally trembling with fear in the waiting area. Pat finally came back and we were called into the doctor's office. She had the images from my mammogram on the light box and I could see both my boobs. It didn't look good to me, both were covered in white blotches. The doctor smiled and said your mammogram is clear and you're fine. No, surely, she's got that wrong. I asked her: "But what about all those white blotches?". "Perfectly normal healthy tissue," she replied. Oh my God, I was so relieved that I just burst into tears. Such rollercoaster emotions, from total fear and anxiety one minute only to be shot back up into total euphoria – it's a wonder I didn't have a heart attack through all of this.

The following year we wanted to go to Mexico for a holiday, but the cost of insurance for me to go was exorbitant because I'd had cancer, even though I was in the clear now. Apparently, I had to wait 5-years and then get the all clear before my insurance premium would drop back to normal. I was fuming! How could they do this? The cost of the insurance was greater than the price of the holiday! I thought it so unfair that insurance companies could penalise people for being ill when they would really benefit from having a holiday. I understood that some people were at higher risk of becoming ill on holiday but surely in my case, and others like me who had their tumours removed and completed treatment, they would wait until they returned home and then contact their own medical team.

Needless to say, we didn't go to Mexico. It took me a while before I realised that although I needed travel insurance, I could opt out of being covered for breast cancer.

In January of the following year I joined our local gym. I needed to lose a bit of weight but more importantly I needed to get fit. All through my treatment year I had not been very active so my fitness levels were at zero. I huffed and puffed just climbing a flight of stairs. I went to the gym 3-4 times a week and slowly I noticed improvement. Although I wasn't losing too much weight, by body was changing shape and becoming firmer. I decided I would enter the Race for Life that year, so I had a real incentive to get fit.

The Race for Life is part of Cancer Research UK and raises money for breast cancer research. They hold an annual event, usually in June, in various locations across the country where entrants can walk, jog or run 5K to raise valuable funds. I entered in 2007 and my target was to raise £100. Pat decided to do it too and we had another friend who wanted to take part as her daughter was going through breast cancer treatment at the time. We ordered the fund-raising packs and bought the T-shirts. Our event took place on a lovely warm Saturday morning in Oxford. The atmosphere was amazing. There were thousands of people, mainly women, wearing pink with dedications to their loved ones affected by breast cancer on the back of their T-shirts. Some of the ladies were still going through treatment and dealing with its effects, some in wheelchairs being pushed around the course - all determined to take part. It was a very moving experience. That was the furthest I had walked in one go since before diagnosis and I was so glad to cross that finish line. We even got a medal. We went off to the pub after that for a lovely lunch and an afternoon spent with fabulous friends. In total, I raised around £1,500 for the charity.

About a year after treatment had finished I decided I wanted to live a bit more. I needed more fun in my life, after all I had just come through a life-threatening illness! We had some friends who belonged to a local social club so we decided to join. I must say here that this was totally my idea and I pushed for it. I don't think Pat and Geoff were too keen, but Pat said she would come with me and eventually Geoff joined too. The Club was a typical British social club with a comfy seating area, a dance floor, subsidised bar and even a snooker room. Every Saturday night a band played live music and we would go, meet up with friends and dance the night away. I became quite addicted and lived for my Saturday nights. I will admit that I drank far too much alcohol during this time and my eating was getting a little out of control too and I gained a lot of weight. Nevertheless, I was happy and I felt so alive. I remember one particular New Year's Eve, the band was particularly good, everyone was happy and ready to enjoy themselves. Midnight hit and we formed our circle and sang Auld Lang Syne. The emotions rolled over me in waves. I was alive. I was about to move into a brand-new year. I had made it. I cried. I stood in that circle and cried tears of pure joy, relief, and happiness.

The partying went on for quite a few years. Not only did we go the Club every Saturday night, I was also up for any other social event and hardly ever refused an invitation. Life was for living and I intended to live it to the full. Eventually, though, I realised that this lifestyle couldn't go on forever. I was drinking and eating far too much and a recent blood test and scan revealed I had developed a fatty liver. Something had to change. I joined Weight Watchers and started to lose weight, I reduced the amount of alcohol I drank, I started walking more. We stopped going to the Club as often and although I wasn't happy about it, I realised that it had to be done. I don't think Pat and Geoff were too sorry, and I know that my drinking caused Pat concern.

And so, the years rolled on. I continued with hospital check-ups, which were all fine, and eventually, 5-years later, I was discharged. Again, I was both elated that it was over but still held that lingering fear of the cancer returning and, to be honest, I was scared that I was on my own with no checks. I developed an almost irrational fear of believing that every little twinge in my body was the cancer returning. Was I becoming a raving hypochondriac? I grew to understand that the fear would never completely go away, but it did diminish.

I spent a long time waiting for the old me to return, the woman I was before cancer, the woman who was care-free and lived a life full of fun and enjoyment. I waited and waited for her before realising that she had gone. It was then that the realisation finally hit me. I'd had cancer! I had spent so long coping with the diagnosis and treatments and illness that I never had time to really accept that I was a cancer patient. The full impact of having cancer had never hit home, but it did then and I had to come to terms with it. Yes, I'd had cancer and, yes, I could have died, but I hadn't. I had survived and was still here to enjoy my life. Yes, it was different than before cancer, but that didn't make it worse or better – it was just different. It was down to me to make it better!

There were a few major changes after cancer, all of which proved beneficial. I changed my job which, after 20-odd years, was a big event. The new job was good and I enjoyed it, but I wasn't passionate about it. My passion came a few years later when I started my own business, which I'll tell you more about later.

CANCER THE SECOND TIME

Fourteen years have passed and there were many highs and lows during that time, some of which I will tell you about in the next section, but on the whole, life had been good.

But then the year 2020 arrived and what I thought was going to be a fabulous year went badly wrong when Coronavirus struck. It hit us all hard and by March we were in lockdown in the UK. Businesses were going down the tubes and holidays cancelled, we were no longer allowed to be with family and friends. I'm a real people person and I really miss being with others so much. I miss the hugs! Then, as if all that coronavirus stuff wasn't enough, on the morning of Monday 29th June, I found a lump! It felt as if the whole of my bowel was about to hit the floor. This surely couldn't be happening. *Not again.* I felt my boob again – yes, there it was, nestling just behind the nipple of my right breast. Same side as before. I carried on with my shower and got dressed, and then I started to do the ironing. I wanted today to be just like any other Monday morning, me doing the ironing and not a care in the world. Then Pat walked into the kitchen and took one look at me. "What's the matter?" she asked. "I've found a lump," I asked her to have a feel and she agreed, it was a lump. "Right, phone the doctors now," she said.

I did – mainly because she wouldn't have shut up until I had, but also because I knew it really was the best thing for me to do. But we were in this bloody pandemic situation and getting through to the doctors, especially on a Monday morning, was not easy. I phoned the surgery and got through to the automated answer phone with all the options available. I ended up pressing option 1 for emergencies because I didn't know what else to do. I waited for a while and finally connected with a real live person. I apologised for using the emergency option but explained that I'd found a lump and that I'd had breast cancer before. I got an appointment with a doctor within 20-minutes! Wow, that's extremely rare, usually, you have to wait a week or two. A good start, someone was on my side.

The doctor examined me, felt the lump but said she couldn't feel anything in my armpit, which was a good sign. She would refer me to the hospital for further checks and then came out with all the right words of not worrying because it could be nothing. *Don't worry, my arse! How could I not worry – this was happening to me a second time.* I wasn't just worrying, I was shit scared. I went home to wait and so the journey began again.

I usually do a Zoom call with Gill, my business partner and best friend, every Monday morning. We message one another daily, but Monday mornings we get to see each other too. Once we went into lockdown in March we had to alter the way we worked and all our group sessions moved over to Zoom. I didn't like not being with people, and I missed seeing and working with Gill, but we had no choice. Everyone's safety was priority and anyway, this would be over soon and we could get back to normal. I messaged Gill early to say I was at the doctors and would let her know when I was home. When we eventually connected on Zoom she immediately said: "what's wrong, why were you at the doctors?" I told her about the lump and she was, for a moment, shocked into silence. Now Gill doesn't do silent, and especially not in the morning. But she soon found her voice and said: "it will be fine, you will be fine because I am not losing you yet," and then we both cried.

The hospital phoned within the week and gave me a date. The lady apologised for the delay but said that there was a backlog because of Covid. My appointment date was set for 19 July, just a little over two weeks since my GP visit.

Hospital day and it's all different. Because of the Covid pandemic I had to do it alone, no family or friends unless you needed special assistance. Before I even got into the department I had to be temperature checked, answer a load of questions, sanitise my hands, and have a clean mask in place. It was the same waiting room as 14-years earlier, but this time there were just single chairs spaced apart, maintaining social distancing. The waiting room was fairly full and I sat in my own little bubble of fear. I know they have to do it, but I felt so alone. I didn't want to do this, I wasn't even sure that I could do it again. Deep breaths in and let them go slowly. You can do this, you're stronger than you think, you've got this. Deep breath in, and release.

As always, I had a long wait but I finally saw a doctor, a lovely bubbly Italian lady. She asked me loads of questions, examined me, and said that she was quietly optimistic about the whole thing but would send me for a mammogram, scan, and possible biopsy if the mammogram showed it to be a new thing. There was another long wait. All I wanted was to go home! Home is safe, home is secure. I don't know why I think that because bad things can happen there too, but I feel safer at home.

Eventually I had the mammogram and it obviously showed the lump as a new thing because I had to wait for a scan. I was finally called in and the scan done. The woman there said there was nothing in the armpit and she didn't think it was a cancer. However, just to be sure she would do a biopsy. I'd had a biopsy before so I knew what to expect and I was quite relaxed. The worse thing about it was the local anaesthetic, but the biopsy didn't hurt and it was soon over. I was free to go home to my safe place.

I felt fairly relieved because the news wasn't all that bad. The doctor was quietly optimistic and the woman doing the scan said she didn't think it was cancer, so I was feeling ok. There was still the thought in the back of my mind of "what if?" but I didn't dwell on it. I had a couple of weeks to wait for the results.

I became very much focused in the moment, not trying to think too much about the what ifs. I took it one day at a time, living in the now. It's really difficult to do that at the best of times, let alone when something major is cropping up in your life, but that's exactly the time you need it the most. One thing I did know for sure was that there would be no way I was going through chemotherapy again. Once I had made that decision not to have chemotherapy it was like a great weight had been lifted. This was my decision to make this time and I was not going to be bamboozled into having treatment that I didn't want.

I told Pat and Gill that chemo was not and never would be an option for me but got the impression that they were not 100% happy with that news. I know they want me alive, whatever it takes, but there is no way I am doing chemo again. I hope they come around to my way of thinking because I do need their support with whatever decision I make, but I will make this decision with or without their support. But hey, that was still a way off yet and I might not have to even make that decision. One day at a time. Oh, how I hated those words the last time. Everyone told me to take it one step at a time and I wanted to punch them in the face. One step at a time – this was my life we were talking about!

I started a new journal. One of the things I find really helpful in my life now is journaling, writing about what's happening and the thoughts, feelings and emotions surrounding that event. It's important to get all of that out rather than bottling it up and have it come back and bite you on the bum at some future date. My journal is private, and that allows me to be totally honest in what I write. It helps me sometimes to see things in a clearer perspective and helps to keep a balance. Who knows, one day I might turn it into a book!!!

- WAITING FOR ANSWERS -

I hate the waiting, it's almost the worse thing of all. There's nothing

I can do except sit and imagine. What if, what if, what if?

I tried to keep busy but that wasn't really helping. Last time I still worked full time so had a lot to occupy both my time and my mind. This time, however, because of Covid our business had almost ground to a halt. Even though we were out of lockdown, our Government still wanted us to keep our distance and not gather in large numbers. We continued to run some of our group sessions on Zoom and still offered training courses in smaller numbers but it seemed there was a general reluctance to use Zoom and book training. It could have been for financial reasons of course, but it was a very quiet time with very little for me to do. So, I found myself wallowing more in the what ifs.

I was supposed to be living in the now and maintaining positive thoughts. I knew how much that helped and I knew that it worked. It's something I taught to my students with great results but I must admit that it all seemed so airy fairy to me at the moment. I wanted something more to do but I didn't know what. I wish this had never happened, I wish I was ok, I wish it was 6-months from now. Oh, I wish, I wish, I wish.

Finally, the hospital appointment arrived. It was the 22nd July: the day I would get the results. It was the day I both dreaded but wanted at the same time. It was the day that I would know one way or the other and I hoped to God it was not bad news. The one thing I did know was that living with not knowing was a living hell. It gave my mind free reign to conjure up all sorts of scenarios. I couldn't live like that for much longer or I would have gone insane. Anyway, even if it was cancer I was not having chemo again – end of story!

Once more I went through the Covid checks and then I sat in that dreaded waiting room for over an hour. All of us in our own little bubbles, physically separated but united by fear. Eventually, I was called. A new room and a new doctor. He had a student with him and asked if I was happy with that and then faffed about on his computer. Both wore masks so it was very difficult to read their faces! I sat in fear and anticipation but still he faffed. I asked him if it was good or bad, and he just said he needed to get the results up on screen. His bloody faffing went on forever and I could have smacked him. Then a nurse came into the room and sat down. He introduced her as Ginny the Breast Care Nurse and then I knew. "It's bad news, isn't it?" I said. "Well", he said, "it's not all completely bad."

It's cancer!!! Triple negative as before but with a percentage of hormonal too. This time I would have a mastectomy and then they will decide what follow-up treatment is needed. I needed to have CT and MRI scans just to see if it's spread anywhere else in my body but, at the moment, the armpit and lymph nodes seem clear. As the cancer is the same type as last time, they will refer me to genetics for screening. Dates for the scans and surgery would be sent to me but all would take place within the next 2-3 weeks.

I told him at that point that I would not be having chemotherapy and he replied: "let's just wait and see what we're dealing with here." He told me that my past chemo worked well for me and gave me 14-years of being cancer-free, so that is what he's aiming for again. *Chemo worked well for me my arse.* He didn't know the half, and neither did he want to know.

I didn't warm up to that man and it wasn't just because he gave me bad news. He seemed cold and aloof – I was simply another patient, another number on his list. Ginny, on the other hand, was lovely and took me off to another room where we could sit and chat. She told me that things had changed a lot in the past 14-years and again just reinforced that I should wait and see before making a final decision on chemotherapy. Mmmmmm – still not changing my decision.

For my mastectomy, I would go to The Manor, a private hospital in Oxford. I would be a day case so presuming all goes well will be home that evening. Internal stitches in the wound, the external will be glued and no drain! I would be given a softie to wear inside a bra and my fitting for a prosthesis would be 6-8 weeks after surgery, giving the wound time to heal.

I left the hospital with an armful of pamphlets and other literature about breast cancer and put them all straight in a drawer when I got home. Obviously not happy, but Pat was fabulous and reassured me that we would get through this, whatever happened. Gill was great too, we still had our Monday chats and some weeks we would cry and some weeks we would laugh. Gill held the space for me to let out all my emotions in a loving and safe environment. She allowed me to voice the fears that I felt I couldn't say to Pat. Pat had her own fears and she wasn't voicing any of them!

In the following days, I went to some very dark places. Now I'm not afraid of dying at all because I know I'll go to a better place, but I didn't want to die yet. What frightened me more was being ill and a long painful lingering death. My mind, or ego, was my own worst enemy and it was continuously feeding me worse case scenarios. I've named my ego Elsie and on several occasions, I told her to fuck off. She told me of all the horrible things that were going to happen whilst I tried my hardest to remain positive. One thing was still for sure – I was not having chemo again.

Now was the time I had to tell Jordan. I really didn't want to but he would have been angry with me if I didn't. I sent him a quick message saying I wanted to talk. We eventually had a Skype call and I just told him without beating about the bush. He was shocked, stunned, and upset. Like all Mums, I tried to keep it positive and upbeat but I did cry a bit and so did he. He said he was glad I had told him because he had a need to support and help me through this time. I never thought of it from his point of view. I guess it's the Mum thing to want to protect and shield your kids from the harsh realities of life, even when they're grown up and living away from home. Once I understood his needs, I knew that I had to share the journey with him. He said he felt a bit useless being so far away from home and not being able to be with me. But I know that we can video call any time we want so that is fine. Of course, I wished he was here, I missed him dreadfully but my peace of mind came from the fact that he was safe and in a relatively low Covid area.

Now I knew for sure that it was cancer, I needed to move into some sort of action. I've started self-healing every night, sending in the troops to contain the tumour and boost my white cells. I talked to my Angels and the support they gave me was amazing. I felt that someone had my back. If ever there was a time to turn to my spirituality it was then. It was more than just a faith with me, it is what I know to be true. I have a lot of tools in my toolbox and I will rummage through and use whatever feels right for me. I knew I would be guided, and I would take notice of my own intuition.

Guidance came within a few days when I stumbled across an on-line seminar being given by Bruce Lipton and Gregg Braden about how our own cells can heal our body. I didn't think too much about it at the time, but for some reason I saved that post. I've heard of both Bruce Lipton and Gregg Braden but didn't know much about their work. I'm a firm believer that things cross your path for a reason, so I had to wonder why this was being flagged up to me and why I had instinctively saved it.

Basically, it was a 10-hour on-line seminar talking about how we can work with our cells and release their potential to help heal ourselves. It claimed that Gregg Braden had already healed himself of cancer, but I didn't know whether that was true or not. I knew I had to formulate a plan, work with the knowledge I had and what cropped up for me because one thing was for sure, I was not having chemotherapy again!

The seminar cost $129 (roughly £100) and I bought it! I thought this could be a bit of a game-changer although Elsie Ego told me otherwise. Oh, just sod off Elsie, talk to me when you're in a better mood. I had nothing to lose except $129, but from the moment I hit that Buy Now button I started to feel much better and more positive. I was doing something proactive for myself, even if it was just watching a seminar.

- THE START OF TREATMENT -

Ginny, my breast care nurse, was lovely. She phoned with dates for the MRI and CT scans, the pre-op assessment, and surgery. Wow, how things had changed over the past 14-years – private hospital, day patient, no stitches or drains. Although I was delighted to be a day patient I must admit I was a bit concerned about going home so quickly after such big surgery. I did feel a bit special going to a private hospital though.

I was okay with having the mastectomy and wouldn't have wanted anything different. In fact, I asked the faffing doctor if he would do a double, but the answer was no, he didn't want to take away good healthy tissue. Well, that's all very well for him to make that decision, he didn't have to live with the fear of the cancer returning in that breast. Neither did he have to live with one boob and a falsie stuck in his bra. I did wonder what I would look like after surgery, but I had seen photos, so I had a rough idea. Not a pretty sight but nevertheless it was a small price to pay to be cancer-free and not having to worry about it returning there.

My right boob had served me well over the years, given me lots of pleasure, fed my baby, and filled out clothes nicely but it was now time to say thank you very much and goodbye.

The two scans and pre-assessment went well, although I was at the hospital for most of the day just waiting. I wasn't really looking forward to the scans at all. I knew they would have to get a cannula in the arm for the CT scan to inject the dye and Pat told me how horrible the MRI Scan is, but then she's prone to massive exaggeration!

The MRI was done first and although it wasn't the best of experiences, noisy and I had to keep still, it was okay. I just closed my eyes and went off to some beach somewhere. The CT was a bit trickier and it took about 15-minutes to get the cannula in but was eventually done. I'm beginning to get quite a thing about needles, it's not the actual needle but simply getting them in a vein.

I had a really long wait for the pre-assessment. God knows why, there was no-one else waiting! Eventually called and I answered all the questions correctly and the EEG showed no problems with my heart – always a good sign. I needed to have some bloods taken, but basically I was good to go for surgery.

Oh no, not blood! Of course, she couldn't get into a vein. She had several goes at it with no luck so she called her colleague. The colleague wasn't faffing about at all and in she went – hooray for competent colleagues. I went back home and had to wait for the results. I was worried about what the scans might show but I was practising mindfulness and carrying on with my normal daily life. But whatever shows up, I am not having chemo.

At the beginning of August I spiralled down to a dark place. My thoughts were constantly consumed by cancer, *what will happen next, what if the cancer has spread, what if I have to have chemo before surgery, what if I die, what if ..., what if ..., what if....*Elsie was having a great time and I seemed powerless to stop her. She was constantly telling me that I had a body that was absolutely riddled with cancer and that I would probably die. I tell you, Elsie was not the friend she thought she was and my constantly telling her to go elsewhere was falling on deaf ears.

My stomach felt bloated, tight, and uncomfortable all the time, and I convinced myself that there was a rapidly growing tumour in there. I started getting dizzy spells which was horrid. I was thinking about how my family would cope without me, and all the things I need to do before my demise. I really needed to update my will. I knew I was spiralling downwards and, for a short while, I didn't know what to do. I felt totally lost. I needed to get those thoughts out of my head because as sure as hell they would eventually destroy me, one way or another.

I was spending most of my time in battle with Elsie. I wish she would just sod off! The trouble with Elsie is that she didn't have enough to do and she seemed to get her kicks out of plaguing me! She continues to be a complete and utter pain in the arse.

A Skype call with Jordan proved to be more beneficial than anything I've tried so far to shut Elsie up. I told him what was happening and how angry I was becoming with Elsie, and that she would just not shut up. "Have you tried making friends with her?" he asked.

Now why the hell would I want to do that when I wanted rid of her? He explained that Elsie was never going away, she was part of me and it was her job to try and keep me safe and warn me when things started to go tits up. Shouting at her would not help, she would just shout back. So, by befriending her we could simply have more of a conversation than a slanging match, and by having a conversation and me listening I might hear something useful that could be of benefit to me.

Ok, I get what he's saying but not sure I want to sit down and have a cup of tea with Elsie. But I gave it a try and boy, what a difference that made. The next time she started I remained calm and rational and simply told her that although I heard what she was saying, this is why that is not going to happen right now.

I urge you to try that approach too. If your mind is plagued by unwanted thoughts then know that it is coming from the ego. Give your ego an identity, befriend him/her, and then politely but firmly tell him/her that you hear what's being said, you can even have a discussion about it, but this is why you can't agree with it at this time and you would prefer not to discuss it again.

After I had my first civil conversation with Elsie, and she did in fact back off a little, I decided I needed to do some meditation. I went into my heart space. It's a beautiful place, loving and peaceful and I know I need to spend more time there. I must plan to spend some time every day doing some sort of meditation. Afterwards I felt quite light-headed, but ok.

The following day I felt a little lighter. I knew these waves of emotions and feelings were normal and just passing through. I tried to accept them as just that, but that's not easy. The physical discomfort was horrible and serves to remind me just how powerful the mind is.

I want to cope with this health issue in my own way, but I need to be strong and do what's right for me.

- FEELING MORE POSITIVE -

I had a bad week with ups and downs, mostly downs. I had physical symptoms that took me to dark places, but yesterday saw a major shift. Befriending Elsie and meditating has had a profound effect. I spent most of the day in the garden enjoying the beautiful warm weather. I listened to the Audible version of The Spontaneous Healing of Belief by Gregg Braden and it made perfect sense to me. I couldn't claim to understand it all (yet!) but I got the gist of it and that's at least a start.

My Breast Care nurse phoned just to say that all was well for surgery and that if anything was wrong with the blood tests I would have heard by now. I hope she meant with the scans too, but I was optimistic.

For the first time in a week I enjoyed my dinner and ate it all. *Right, I can do this. I have the resources and the ability, I've got this.*

Another Skype call with Jordan and more of his wisdom. I must just say here how very proud of him I am, he really is my guru!! Yeah, ok, it's a Mum thing I know, but I really am proud of the man he's turned out to be.

We talked about my self-healing regime and how it's building up in stages. He's fully supportive but asked why I thought I had to do it in stages and why I didn't think I could go straight in and say: "I am healed"? A true moment of magic occurred – why indeed? I know that energetically everything happens in the moment, in the now! So why on earth was I faffing about in stages? No, no, no, no, no – I want to be healed so healed I am. The moment I thought *"I am healed"* it is done, my healing has already happened.

The following morning, I woke up with cramp in my foot. Normally I would wriggle my foot, stretch it, get out of bed, stomp it on the floor and dance around the bedroom. There's almost a kind of panic when cramp sets in – there's a need to get rid of it as quickly as possible. What on earth do we think will happen if we didn't get rid of it sooner than immediately? Would my foot end up deformed?

That morning I tried a different approach. All my instincts were saying "stomp around the bedroom", but that morning I used thought energy. In my mind, I simply thought: "the cramp has gone" and it went – instantly. So, the same principle must apply to any other condition – intend it to be gone and it's gone. Our own limiting beliefs lead us think that the bigger the condition the less likely we are to heal it ourselves. Totally not true – the same principle applies!

I mentioned earlier that I was keeping a journal. Now I end each entry with "I AM HEALED". It's my affirmation that it's already happened. Affirmations are good things to adopt. Choose one every day and when you start to get a bit wobbly and begin to dwell on the negative stuff, just repeat your affirmation over and over in your mind. You can say it out loud if you like, but anyone around you might think you have lost the plot!

- SURGERY WEEK -

It's Monday morning mid-August and the week that I've both been dreading and waiting for at the same time. The week of surgery but before I got that far I needed to have a Covid test, an injection to track to the lymph node and I had to meet my surgeon. Ginny has already told me who it would be and the girls have told me he's gorgeous. We refer to him now as the Gorgeous One!

Monday morning came and off I went to the hospital for a Covid test. I was sure it would be ok but, as with any test, you still wonder: what if? I didn't want this surgery cancelled for any reason. Although I didn't want to have it, I needed to get rid of the tumour from my body.

The test was done at the hospital and was a drive-through arrangement. Although not pleasant – I mean that swab is long and they shove it right up the nose and so far down the throat I started to gag – but it was quick and I was soon off home. One thing ticked off the list!

Tuesday morning and back to the hospital. First up was the dye injected into the breast which would track its way to the lymph node. Not looking forward to that much. Will it hurt? I'm a bit of a baby where pain is concerned. The injection was quick and painless. Why on earth did I worry about that? The nurse popped it into the breast just behind the nipple, whereas in my mind I thought it was going straight into the lymph node. Oh, a little knowledge is such a dangerous thing!

Next up was meeting the Gorgeous One and I wondered whether he would be as gorgeous as they all say? Even the nurses think he's gorgeous. I should know more about the results of my scans. Did I want to know? Yes and no. But I had to know because living with not knowing is the worst thing of all. It leaves ample room for Elsie to get her two-bobs worth in.

Was it a coincidence that my surgeon was called Dennis, the same name as my late husband? No, I don't believe in coincidences, it's all synchronicity. My husband will be watching over me because I do believe he continued to love me despite all that happened between us and the parting of the ways.

The Gorgeous One came in and yes, he really was gorgeous. I couldn't see all his face because of the mask but lovely dark brown eyes framed by oodles of dark lashes that any woman would give her right arm for. Those eyes smiled a lot too. Not only was he easy to look at but his personality matched. He was easy to talk to and he listened, he really listened and he heard me. He told me my scans were clear and was both surprised and a bit miffed that no-one had phoned with those results. He actually made me look on his computer screen so I could see for myself. Total relief flooded through me. My Covid test was also negative.

He ran through the surgery with me. He said that due to the internal scarring from previous surgery and the radiotherapy that I'd had, he couldn't go as close to the chest wall as he normally would. I would be left with a little excess skin but assured me that it wouldn't be all saggy and once healed it would be fine. I would go home the same evening as surgery, providing all was well and I would receive a follow-up appointment for a couple of weeks, by video call, to discuss the results.

I left the hospital feeling very happy. My scans were clear and I liked my surgeon, I had faith in him and I trusted him. I was so grateful.

Next up was surgery on Thursday and I felt ok with that. I had not given too much thought to losing my boob, I was thinking more about getting rid of the tumour. I was sure I would be a bit of a wreck on Thursday morning, but I knew I would get through it. Often the waiting is worse than getting on and doing it. I was still very much determined to do things my way. I wanted to live a much healthier life from now on. I wouldn't flood my body with copious amounts of red wine anymore but would still enjoy the odd glass of something. I would also eat more fresh fruit and vegetables, organic would be lovely. I would continue to walk whenever I could. I was looking forward to Friday and it all being over.

During a Skype call with Jordan he voiced his concerns over my chosen route versus chemotherapy. He asked if I was just being stubborn old me and not wavering from a decision rather than giving chemotherapy careful consideration. I understood what he was saying. He didn't want me to die and he had conventional medicine hard-wired into his subconscious. I must admit that the conversation made me have a moment or two of doubt, and I started to wonder if I was taking the easier option to avoid the pain and illness of chemo.

But clarity reigned the next morning. I was actually taking the harder option by taking a leap of faith. I was sure the oncologist would give me all the statistics as to why I should go the chemo route, or any other kind of drug therapy, and he would always go for the best option based on statistics. But he didn't know what I was like with chemo last time!

This time, I was opting to trust in my belief that there is a greater force at play and that we all have the potential to do great things.

This was the harder option because I was putting all my trust in the unknown and at the moment, that was totally outside of my reality. I was determined to make it my reality but it would take commitment and trust. I was focusing on the outcome, of what I want to happen. I'm not saying it is easy, in fact, it's bloody hard and I was scared. But what did I have to lose? Well, my life. But I was going to die at some point anyway! Dying didn't scare me, it would be a wonderful new adventure. But the journey towards death did scare me.

But that won't happen for a long while yet because I've got stuff to do before I go. Finish this book for one thing! And anyway, I am healed!

- SURGERY -

I spoke to Jordan the day before surgery and told him the results of scans. He was absolutely delighted that everything was going well and totally supportive of everything that I was doing to help myself. Whenever I had good results he referred to it as 'more of Mum's Magic'. Indeed, that's exactly what it felt like. I spent time quietly visualising the outcome I wanted and most of the time I lived as if it had already happened. Elsie sometimes piped up with one of her 'ah yeah, but ...' quips, but I was quick to thank her and tell her firmly that we would not be having that conversation. My relationship with Elsie had vastly improved and, although she hadn't gone away, she was far less insistent than she used to be.

The day of surgery dawned and I had to be at the hospital by 7am. I hoped I would be first on the list to get it over with. I had my own room with a bathroom. It was minimal but adequate. I was given a hospital gown to wear, some very sexy mesh knickers and a pair of flattering white knee-high elastic socks. What a sight! All the routine pre-surgery checks were done and one of the surgeons popped in and drew lines and arrows over my boob with a black marker pen. He told me I was first on the list and would be going to theatre around 9am.

I actually walked down to theatre and got on the table myself. All very daunting but everyone was lovely, but would you believe it - the anaesthetist couldn't get into a vein. Oh bloody hell, this was my worst nightmare! How on earth would they knock me out if they couldn't get into a vein. He must have seen the panic in my eyes because he told me not to worry, he would go into the right arm (the one he couldn't use because it was the side of surgery) to get me off to sleep and then find a vein once I was out of it. I had an overwhelming urge to shout stop and get off the table and go home. 'Come on girl, get a grip,' I thought and then I called my Angels. If ever I needed them it was now.

A sense of calm washed over me and the next thing I knew was waking up in recovery and it was all over. True to his word the anaesthetist had found another vein - in my left foot. Back in my room I was given a cup of tea and some lunch. I slept on and off and then towards the end of the afternoon the Gorgeous One came in and told me that it all went well, no drain and no external stitches and I could go home. Once again, I was ecstatic. I could have kissed him. I was desperate to get home, I felt fine and not in any pain.

I decided to get dressed in the bathroom. There was a big mirror over the sink, and I thought the sooner I looked at the scar the better. It had to be done and I wanted to do it whilst I was alone so my reaction couldn't be witnessed. I took the hospital gown off and just stared. Not only had my right breast suddenly disappeared, the scar was ugly. It looked like a lopped-sided smiley face, the scar itself was puckered and was covered in a mauve coloured glue. I sighed, is this it? Is this what I will look like from now on? I had a moment or two of sadness. After nearly 60-years of seeing myself with two boobs and now only seeing one was not a nice experience. The old me had gone and I could never get her back. It was very similar to looking into the mirror after chemo had taken all my hair – who was this woman looking back at me? Where had I gone? I was facing a different future and I had to learn a new way to be. But then would you believe Elsie kicked in with some wise words that I would never have thought possible. Yes, it's ugly now but would improve with time, but the main thing was that the cancer had been cut away. I was now cancer free! I actually smiled and thanked her.

I was home again. What a relief! It was all over, I could start the recovery process. I was a little uncomfortable in bed that night but my lovely friend Linda had bought me a Cushtie Pillow in my favourite colour, pink. That Cushtie was just the best thing ever and supported my arm and kept it away from my chest. I didn't sleep too well that night, not because of the pain but I was reliving the events of the day but apart from that first night, I began to sleep really well.

A few days after surgery and I experienced my first emotional outburst since this whole journey began. I was trying to explain to Pat how I felt the first time I looked in the mirror and saw my scar. I felt she wasn't hearing me. Oh, she was listening to me but she wouldn't really let me talk, she kept coming back with all the right things to say to try and make me feel better. I totally understand her, I've probably done the same thing many times in the past, but sometimes I just need someone to really hear what I'm saying and to empathise. It really is true that you can never really understand someone and their situation until you have experienced it for yourself. Please Angels, don't ever let her experience this!

But as we were talking, Geoff walked into the room and sat down and started burbling on about something totally trivial. He just didn't understand that this was a private moment and he never saw that I was getting upset. I never finished what I wanted to say. I just pushed it all back down again. The crunch came a few minutes later when I tried to order a couple of soft bras on-line. All I wanted was a couple of soft, front-fastening bras with pockets in either white or skin tones, not too expensive and not taking two months to arrive. That should have been easy but proved almost impossible, and that was my trigger. Pat didn't understand what all the fuss was about and got quite cross with me.

"Just order a couple of bloody bras!" she snapped. I cried. Again, she wasn't hearing me. Geoff came into the room again and started adding his two-penny worth, so I yelled at him.

Why, oh, why don't they hear me? Why can't they realise that they can't make this better? This is how I'm going to look for the rest of my life. I cried it out and then went off and did my exercises.

After that outburst, I felt much better. I understood that I would have them from time to time and that they were all part of the process and I needed to accept them as part of the healing journey. I'm working my way through saying goodbye to my old body and welcoming the new. It's a kind of grieving process. Whether I like it or not, this is me. Lopping off my boob doesn't make me any less of the person I was.

- RECOVERY -

Recovery went well. I did my daily self-healing and meditation and got plenty of rest. I also did the exercises that the physiotherapist gave me in the hospital to get full movement back in the arm and shoulder as quickly as possible. I slowly regained my strength in my right arm and was enjoying life again. I lived bra-less around the house and was getting used to the way I looked. I didn't particularly like having only one boob, which seemed to double in size overnight and I also seemed to develop the added attraction of a buddha-belly! I was eager to get my prosthesis so that I could even things up – a typical Libran, I needed balance. I was given a softie to wear but, to be honest, it was pretty useless and I couldn't seem to get it looking even inside my very soft bra.

I was taking each day as it came, I was relaxed and happy and enjoying the time with nothing much to do. I started to work on myself with healing, meditating and visualisation. The next step was to have a video call with my surgeon to get the results of surgery, so I used that time to visualise what I wanted the outcome to be. I visualised his face on my computer screen telling me that all was well, results were fine and no further treatment necessary. I held onto that for the next couple of weeks.

Two weeks later and I had a video call with the Gorgeous One. Naturally, I was worried. What would the results of the tissue analysis be? It was strange to think that my breast had been removed and someone somewhere would be looking at it down a microscope. Was it in tact, I wondered, or did the Gorgeous One remove it bit by bit. Was the nipple looking someone right in the eye? Oh, the mind has the strangest of thoughts at times.

The Gorgeous One appeared on screen and this time without a mask so I got a full frontal!! Such a smiling face too. The results were great, the tumour was smaller than expected but was indeed triple negative stage 3 with an element of hormonal in there too. Only one lymph node removed and that was clear. Add to that the clear scans and he was able to confirm that I was indeed cancer-free. I had developed a seroma in the two weeks since surgery, which was sloshing around like a water bath, but it wasn't too big or painful so no need to have it drained. An appointment would be made for me to see the oncologist who would go through the follow-up treatment, which included chemotherapy, hormone therapy and a drug used for the bones which had been shown to give a level of protection for breast cancer.

"I'm not having chemotherapy," I said immediately. "Ok," the Gorgeous One replied. "I hear you, and nobody will make you do anything that you don't want to, but please go along to the meeting with an open mind and listen to what they have to say. " I promised I would – but I'm still not having chemo!!

So, whilst I had wanted him to tell me that all was well and no further treatment needed, the results were still good! The tumour turned out to be smaller than they expected so I had to wonder whether the self-work that I was doing had actually began to shrink the tumour. More of Mum's Magic?

I waited another month for my oncology appointment. During that month, I continued to heal well, the glue was falling off the wound but it was still fairly ugly. I had a little discomfort but no pain. I only needed two painkillers during the whole period which was just a well as they come hand in hand with constipation! I have full range of movement back in my arm and shoulder, so much so that I soon dispensed with the exercises.

Life was good, I was healing well and I had started to go out walking again. Pat and I usually walk 2-3 miles every day when we can and I missed the exercise and fresh air. I still need to get through the Oncology appointment and convince him that I was not having chemo again, but that would be it.

However, emotional healing was taking a little longer. The more I healed physically the more I wanted to get back to normal again, and that's more to do with looks than anything else. I tried an old bra on yesterday with the softie inside. It took ages to get a shape that was anywhere near presentable – I took stuffing out, I put the stuffing back in, I pushed and pulled it around all over the place to try and get an even look and smooth out the lumps. I only wanted to wear it when I went out walking to stop the remaining boob from wobbling about all over the place. It was summer so I was still in T-shirts, one huge wobbly boob and one flat side was a very eye-catching look. To be honest, a double mastectomy would have been better to cope with.

Oh my, I do seem like I do nothing but moan, don't I? But honestly, my days were mostly good with the odd little blip. Pat says I am very childish and she expects me to stamp my feet at any minute. That may well come! I'm sure that everything will be better when I get my proper prosthesis.

- A SOCIAL EVENT -

We were invited to a neighbours coffee morning in aid of the MacMillan charity. I was really looking forward to it. It was my first social occasion in months. I decided to wear a bra and had another performance with it! The bras I had finally bought after my first spectacular meltdown turned out to be bloody useless. They were supposed to have pockets but they were more like flaps. Honestly, they wouldn't have held a pocket-sized handkerchief for a fairy let alone the bloody massive softie that I was given. Ok, I needed to move swiftly along. There is no point dwelling and getting angry, and anyway the new bras made me feel like I had been trussed up a harness. I went back to the soft bra that I had bought from Sainsburys years ago and with a bit of dismantling and restuffing of the softie it was finally in. I had to pin it in place so it didn't pop out the top, but once I put a top over it I didn't look too bad. Hopefully nobody would be staring at my chest. The morning was lovely and it was great to sit and chat with neighbours again. I chatted with one neighbour who was going through bowel cancer and that made me realise that I was not alone, everyone had their issues in one form or another.

Can you believe that as soon as we got home from the MacMillan Coffee Morning the delightful Elsie Ego raised her head again and was trying to convince me that I now had bowel cancer!! I think she picked that idea up from the neighbor I was chatting to. It's all based on the fact that every now and then I have a twinge low down on my right side and my ability to poo regularly is abysmal. Personally, I think the twinge is from scar tissue from two previous surgeries and I've always had a problem with going to the loo. I can go for days with nothing occurring. I also have Irritable Bowel Syndrome (IBS) which tends to flare up during times of stress and I think it's fair to say that I've been a bit stressed over the past couple of months. I reminded Elsie of all of that and the fact that my scans were clear, but she was determined to have her say.

"Ah well," she said, "they won't find anything if they're not specifically looking for it." She is unbelievable. I didn't react, just sent her on her way and got myself in the chill zone.

One morning I stood and looked in the bathroom mirror, and really looked for the first time. Oh, I had seen it before of course, but it had always been a scar, a wound, a lost breast, a flat chest. I saw it in isolation. Today, I stood and looked at me with one breast, and I really looked at me.

Ok, no, it wasn't a pretty sight. The scar was still fresh and raw, puckered and ugly. My body is overweight and full of lumps and bumps which seem to show up even more now without my right boob to hide them and provide balance. I'm not a young woman: I'm in my late 60s, and have grey hair and wrinkles. I need glasses because I'm half blind without them and, if truth be told, I would probably benefit from hearing aids. But in that woman who stared back at me from the mirror I saw a kind of beauty. Physically she was flawed, but it didn't matter. I saw her strength and I saw a kind of defiance – this is who she was, take her or leave her, love her or hate her because she wasn't changing for anyone and she certainly wasn't hiding away or being anything less than who she was. Her spirit was whole, intact and, if anything, stronger because of her experiences. I am learning to love this woman.

- ONCOLOGY -

Hospital appointment day and I went off to oncology prepared for a fight. I felt they would try to convince me to have all sorts of treatment and I really didn't want to fight.

Well, I got that totally wrong. I saw two great doctors, the first one young and doing all the preliminary stuff. He gave me the statistics and then told me of the three options that were open to me, chemotherapy, hormone therapy and a drug primarily for the bones but which has been shown to give some protection against breast cancer. However, according to the statistics that would only help 1% of women. For me, the risks of having chemotherapy far outweighed the benefits with only a 4% chance of still being alive in 10-year's time. He gave me the percentages for the other treatments and, taken in total, they amounted to 10%. I had a 22% risk of dying from a non-cancer related illness within the next 10-years. There was no way I was going to put my body through all the side effects of those drugs only to be run over by a bus!

It really was a no-brainer for me so I thanked him for the offer of treatment but declined. Based on the statistics, I would be better off with no follow-on treatment and not have to suffer the side effects and any long-term consequences. I had to see the consultant too and whilst he accepted that I didn't want chemotherapy, he did suggest that hormone treatment might be beneficial in protecting the other breast. I asked him about the side effects and the ones he reeled off included nausea, joint and muscle aches, vaginal dryness, hot sweats. He also said I would need regular bone scans as bone density could be affected. He offered me a trial run and if I didn't tolerate it well I could come off it. I really didn't fancy any of that either so we agreed that I would wait until the results of genetic testing came back. If the results were positive and I opted for the second mastectomy then I wouldn't need the drugs. He would see me again in 3-months and then in 6-months after which, unless I changed my mind about treatment, he would discharge me.

A different woman walked out of that hospital. I was walking on air. That was it as far as I was concerned – it was over. Just a couple more checks with the oncologist, annual mammograms for 5-years and I would be out the other side once again.

Once I came back down to earth I realised that I still had some healing to do, both physically and emotionally. The wound was doing ok, but it was still ugly with an area towards the top that was really taking its time to heal. Emotionally I am unsure whether I've fully realised what's happened to me over the past few months. I know it has because my body has changed but it's almost like I've been too busy to really give it all too much thought. How stupid is that?

I haven't been busy at all. But the one thing I tend to do is to put on a brave face for everyone else. I come across as a strong and capable woman, the woman that everyone else leans on, and they fail to see that I'm often screaming inside. In fact, the braver the face the more I convince myself that I'm not screaming. I think Pat sees the screaming but doesn't want to go there because quite often she is screaming too. She's excellent with the practical stuff but doesn't do the emotional stuff too well. Jordan sometimes sees the screaming and encourages me to talk, but I'm good at hiding it from him too. Gill often sees it, she lets me talk and she cries with me.

These are the three most important people in my life and they all fulfil different roles and meet my needs. I have another close friend who lets me talk and she gets me because she's been there herself. Thank you Linda. I am so blessed to have them all.

So, whilst my euphoria is dwindling, I am still extremely happy and grateful.

- ONWARDS AND UPWARDS -

Working my way through the books that I had on healing, it seemed that for any illness to manifest in the body there is an external trigger that sets it off. I was convinced that my trigger was stress and is probably the case with a lot of people. For the past several years, I had lived with Pat's second stroke, her sciatica, her skin cancer, her deteriorating eyesight, her seizure and just when her health was beginning to stabilise, my husband and brother-in-law were both found dead in their home. Dealing with their affairs fell to me as there were no other relatives. As if that wasn't quite enough along came coronavirus, the lockdown, the media telling us we were all doomed, and the government running around with their heads up their arses! I will admit to finding the pandemic quite a stressful time and more so because of Pat's health issues.

Jordan and his partner Adelya were living in Thailand at the time and with their visas about to expire, they chose to go to Bali. Not long after arriving there Jordan got sick and I wondered whether he had caught the virus, albeit in a mild form.

It seemed my mind had been filled with fearful thoughts for a long time so it stands to reason that something had to give, didn't it? It was possible that all the fear and stress had manifested itself as breast cancer.

Let me tell you about another emotional outburst and how petty it was but seemed major to me at the time. It was a Sunday morning. The mess lying around the house was beginning to get on my nerves, nobody puts anything away. I made a comment about it and I will admit that I could have put it a bit more tactfully. Geoff never says much, just mutters under his breath, but Pat turned around and told me I was getting on her nerves. Because I was a bit more emotional than usual her quip really hit home. It seemed that she was constantly telling me to go and sit down and I was feeling she didn't have time for me because she had too much to do. I felt that Gill didn't have time for me either because she was so busy with her own work and she had messaged to say she wanted to change the time of our usual Zoom chat. I felt she was just fitting me in. All bloody stupid, I knew that but I think deep down I was feeling lonely and isolated. If it wasn't for this shitting bloody virus I would have taken myself off to see Linda but here I was instead, Billy Bloody No Mates!

I needed a hug and couldn't have one, so I cried instead. How bloody childish of me and so out of character. I realised that after the emotional high of the oncologist appointment, I had to crash down again at some point. What a bloody journey it was, but rather than dwelling on it and feeling worse I decided to do something about it. I told Pat exactly how I was feeling. Yes, I cried a lot but it was such a relief to let those feelings out and I ended up having a lovely day.

The next morning I had a chat with Gill and again, I told her how exactly how I felt. I cried again, and she cried and told me how she had been feeling from when I was first diagnosed. We cried together and I not only felt better after that emotional release, but I felt closer to Gill than ever.

It really does you good to release the worries, anxieties, frustrations, etc that have been building up, but you also need to talk to someone who really hears what you're saying. If you don't have friends or family that you feel you can be totally honest and open with, then do consider joining a support group.

You may be lucky enough to have a support group near you but if not there are some very good ones on social media. This time round I joined one on Facebook that is specifically for those of us who have had mastectomies. It's very friendly, supportive and most of all everyone knows exactly what you're talking about because they have been through it themselves.

Nine weeks after surgery I got itchy feet. We should have been getting ready to go on holiday now but because of the Pandemic it's been cancelled. That's a real bummer because right now I feel I need some fun. I could really do with a good night out and a good laugh. But I realise that these are very strange times right now and we have to keep everyone safe.

At the end of October, I finally made my appointment for the genetics blood test. I've been procrastinating over this because there are consequences. If it's a positive result then I have to talk to Jordan and he has to consider what he needs to do. He will be offered testing here in the UK but, of course, he lives most of the time overseas. If it's positive then I will have the option of having the other breast removed. If the results are negative then no knock-on effect for Jordan and I will have to fight to get the second mastectomy, should I want to go that route. I want a negative result because I don't want to have passed rubbish genes to my son. The results are not due back until early in the new year but with Covid it may well take longer. And so, we wait.

At the beginning of November, the whole country went back into lockdown to try to control the coronavirus and get the numbers down before Christmas. I was so grateful that I managed to get my treatment before this happened as our hospitals and staff are becoming stretched.

I developed a rash underneath my mastectomy wound in mid-November, and the scar itself was ouzing a bit. I phoned my doctors surgery and eventually spoke to a nurse. I had to send photos of the rash and wound, can you believe that? This is the way our medical service is moving now. It's probably due to Covid and the need to keep people away from the surgery, and I totally understand that, but I would have preferred a doctor to actually look at it.

The nurse wasn't sure what it was but gave me a prescription for antibiotics and some cream. A few days later I was chatting with Linda and Pat on a Zoom call and they persuaded me to phone my Breast Care Nurse and get it checked out properly. I phoned and she wanted to see me, so back to the hospital I went. She looked and although there was still some fluid buildup she didn't think there was a problem. She asked me to go back next day and let my surgeon check it. I didn't mind that, I was only too pleased that someone would take a look at it plus I got to see the Gorgeous One again. He looked at it and confirmed that it was nothing to worry about, just a buildup of fluid that was trying to find a way out but it wasn't enough to have it drained. The antibiotics were working and I needed to start massaging the area, working away from the wound. I suppose it was a bit naive of me to think I would sail through it all without some sort of glitch, and if that was all there was then I was really grateful.

- BARBARA -

Finally, after nearly 4-months, I got my prosthesis. The fitting was quick and simple and the woman I saw knew what she was doing. I came home with this thing nestled inside my very soft bra. To say it was ugly is an understatement, it's a big slab of beige silicone and it's heavy. Funnily enough though, once my bra is on it doesn't feel too bad. I only had the very soft bras at the moment, my own boob tends to do its own thing and goes into free-form whereas the prosthesis tends to sink to the bottom of the bra. The measuring lady assured me that a good fitting bra would solve that problem and she gave me the size I needed to buy.

I don't like the word prosthesis, not only do I have difficulty saying it, but it conjures up all sorts of appendages. So, I've called it Barbara. Each night she nestles in her own little box ensuring she maintains her shape. I've been told to wash her with whatever I use to wash my body with, so I take her into the shower with me and give her a good old lathering of Dove body wash, hose her down and then pat her dry with a towel and we're good to go.

I have three different types of soft bra and I've now been through the lot trying to find the best look. Stupidly I thought they would all be absolutely fine, but no! The first was just a little too tight, it squashed the real boob to a semi-flatness, but Barbara was not being squashed at all. She stood proud and strong and, like a beacon, she drew the eye towards her. The second bra was a touch too big and although it allowed real boob a bit more freedom, dear old Babs just sunk to the bottom and hung there. Every time I bent forward Babs would hang like a bloody great melon, making me look like some deformed rhinoceros. The third bra I tried was the best of the bunch, but not perfect by any means. I clearly needed to go shopping. Was finding a natural look always going to be a major problem?

To be perfectly honest, I would prefer to be completely flat. I wish they had done the double mastectomy at the time but the surgeons were adamant that they wouldn't. I know to be flat means more surgery and that's not something I relish but living with one boob is really not good for me and Babs - bless her - is really quite heavy.

So why do I want to be flat? Well, firstly there is the fear that cancer will strike the remaining boob and the constant worry of whether I would catch it early enough to stop it spreading around my body. Fear is an awful thing to live with and can and does cause a lot of physical and emotional damage.

Secondly, there is the psychological impact of how you actually look after surgery and as a woman that is a major issue to deal with. I hate the way I look now. It doesn't cause me too much angst but I would rather not have to think about it at all than constantly faffing about trying to get an even look. I think whatever age we are we all like to look our best and whilst on the outside we may look okay to others, it's how we feel about ourselves that really matters.

Thirdly, there is the issue of trying to look my best. You already know I'm a bit vain and yes, I do have my prosthesis now and it does make me look kind of even, but I have to make sure that I have the right kind of bra to achieve a fairly decent look. When shopping for clothes, I have to consider the shape and the neckline, and horizontal stripes are a definite no-no. All fairly trivial, I know, but it aggravates me that every time I see something I really like it's either too low at the neck, too tight, too eye catching to the chest, etc.

I know there are probably many ladies out there who are totally happy living as a 'uniboober', but my mastectomy has left me feeling irritated. Perhaps it's a time thing and the longer I live like this the more accepting I will become. Please don't misunderstand me, I don't walk round with the ump all the time and I'm totally grateful to still be here fit and healthy, whether I have two, one or no boobs, I just need to regain that feeling good about myself attitude.

- GENETIC TEST RESULTS -

So here we are, at the final part of my story – for now! I don't think I've told you, but if I am repeating myself I apologise just put it down to my age. At my first hospital appointment after I had found the lump, the doctor said she wanted to refer me for genetic testing because of my age and because it was the second lump. It made sense to me and I was ok with that.

My Breast Care Nurse gave me a form to complete which was mainly asking about my family history on both sides of the family. My mother had died when she was 46 from ovarian cancer so I guess there was a stronger possibility that I might have inherited some rogue genes from her, but apart from that there was no strong history of cancer in either side of the family. I completed the form and didn't think too much more of it.

After surgery I had a call from a lovely lady in Genetics who talked me through the whole thing. She had looked at my completed form and agreed that there was more of a risk of me inheriting a mutated gene from Mum that may well have triggered my breast cancers. The test itself was simple enough, a blood test that I could get done at my doctor's surgery. They would send it off to the lab for testing and the results would be back about 6-8 weeks, but could be longer at the moment because of Covid. They would be looking for mutations in three different genes, BRCA1, BRCA2 and PALB2, and if any of these came back positive there would be implications for Jordan and any other close family members.

The implications for me were minimal really. I had already had a full hysterectomy in my 40s so the risk of ovarian cancer had gone. The only thing I could do was have my other breast removed to minimise the risk. To be honest, that wasn't a problem, at least I would be balanced and not have my left boob aimlessly swinging about. The only other close family member was a cousin on my Dad's side of the family who had a daughter and grandchildren, so naturally, I would tell him.

But Jordan was my major concern and my heart ached at having to tell him that I had passed on a rogue gene. The guilt of having done that to him would be another big hurdle for me to deal with. He would be eligible for ongoing screening for breast and prostate cancer, but that was easier said than done when he lived out of the country for much of the time. It would also have big implications for any children that he and Adelya might have, although I was assured that their children would also be screened at the appropriate time.

After that conversation with genetics, and before the paperwork for the blood test came through, I spent every day in meditation working with Joe Dispenza's You Are the Placebo meditation. Every day I worked on changing my genes into good healthy ones. It took about 2-3 weeks for the paperwork to come through for the blood test, and then I procrastinated for another week or so before I made the appointment to get the bloods taken. I figured a month ought to do it to get any rogue genes changed.

Last week Genetics phoned with the results – all negative! Phew, what a relief.

Now I don't know, and I will never know, whether my meditations made any difference to my genes. Pat tells me no, my genes were always my genes, but I'm not so sure.

What do you think?

SPIRITUAL ME

Let me now tell you a little bit about me, what makes me tick and how my life changed considerably from the first cancer journey to the second.

My leaning towards spirituality probably started when I was a kid and my Mum told me that although my granddad had died and couldn't be here with us anymore, he had simply gone to heaven to be with the Angels but was looking down on me and would always be with me. How comforting was that? I was young and had no reason to believe that what she had told me wasn't true. I mean, nobody lies to a kid, do they?

I was born in the early 1950s which, to me, was the best time to come into this world. With my teenage years in the 60s I fully immersed myself in the hippie culture and I was gutted when my parents told me I couldn't go to Woodstock. My first love was John Lennon and even now that I'm older and wiser, I still love that man and all he stood for.

Many years later when I lost my first child I was devastated but I knew that Granddad was in heaven with the Angels so perhaps my baby was there with him too. For some strange reason, I started to read books by the Spiritual Medium Doris Stokes, who specialised in connecting with children in the spirit world. Not only did I find comfort in that but I started to look more into life after death and how it all worked. It really fascinated me and drew me towards learning more.

Then along came the game changer a couple of years later. I was in my twenties at the time and my best friend, June, suggested one day that we go to our local Spiritualist Church. Mainly because we were a bit bored and needed something new in our lives, but also because we wondered what those people did in that spooky place on a Sunday evening. We also thought it would answer all our questions and we would leave the church that night knowing for sure whether there was life after death or not. Oh, the naivety of youth.

It didn't answer a single question but it was a pleasant evening and the people were nice enough, although there was a strange smell about the place, which June insisted was embalming fluid. I mean for heaven's sake how did she even know what embalming fluid smelled like? There was a medium giving out messages but, to be honest, they all seemed a bit vague – of course, your mother is going to be in spirit if you're 87! But we agreed that we would go back until one of us got a message because that was the only way to know for sure. It actually took several months but finally, June got a message. It meant nothing to either of us at the time but her Mum confirmed everything when she phoned her later.

I was pleased she got a message, but I wanted one of my own. We agreed that we would keep going to the church until my message came through. It took another few months of waiting but eventually, it came and I was totally blown away! And that's when my spiritual journey really began.

June and I remained at the Church for several years. The more we went the more we learned about spiritualism which both of us found totally fascinating. We continued to get messages from the weekly visiting mediums; some were really good, some mediocre, and others just plain poor. It's the poor ones that give spiritualism such a bad press. I've no doubt that they believe in what they do and do connect with spirit, but their way of delivering a message is, to be brutal, bloody appalling. Having said that, spirit does not always make it easy to understand what they're on about. But it was the poorer mediums that sometimes made me question what I was doing. What the hell did I think I was playing at, listening to that drivel week in and week out but then every so often an outstanding medium came along and left me in no doubt that we do not die when our bodies do.

By this time, going to the church was so much more than simply getting messages from the dead each week. There was so much to learn, so much to understand and so much to practice if I wanted to go further on my spiritual journey. I was beginning to learn that there was a difference between spiritualism and spirituality and I was on a quest to learn all I could about spirituality and to try and live a more spiritual life.

I joined the Healing Group and went along every Thursday evening. I was shown how to connect with spirit and then place my hands on someone, allowing the healing energy to flow through me to them. I must admit that at the beginning I didn't think this could possibly work and it was all a bit weird. But the first time I placed my hands on someone's shoulders my fingers began to tingle, swell and become tight – they looked like sausages on the ends of my hands. It happened every single time and still happens to this day when I give healing. I had no idea what actually happened in those sessions but the people who came for help went away happy and feeling better.

June and I both wanted to learn how to connect with spirit but there was a reluctance within the older members of the church to teach us. They were old school and thought you had to be a member for donkeys' years before you could progress. Bloody hell, I could be dead by then and it wouldn't matter because then I would know the answers to that which I was seeking. Of course, there were places and people only too willing to teach individuals but that came at a cost and back in those days I didn't have two halfpennies to rub together.

June and I agreed that there was no other way than to do it ourselves. We didn't have a clue on how to go about this but what we did know was that if we sat in the Church, had the right intention, and asked spirit for protection then we couldn't go far wrong – could we? There was a young couple who wanted to learn too so the four of us decided to form our own circle. Once a week we would go into the church, say a prayer of protection and wait to see what happened. We worked purely with our own intuition. I had some very odd experiences during that time and I can remember often feeling so sick that I wondered what point would be the most appropriate for me to run out and vomit! I was told much later that it was just the energy building within me and my body getting used to it.

Eventually we started to connect with spirit and it was as mind-boggling as it was amazing. I was learning a lot and I loved every minute of it.

So, there I was just a few short years later, sitting in circle and doing some healing. Who would have thought it eh? This normal down to earth girl would be rocking with spirit and for once not the alcoholic variety!

- DISRUPTION -

By then I was starting to understand that spirit has more control over our lives than we ever thought possible. Yes, we have our own free will but our guides influence us and steer us in the right direction for our own progression. Looking back now I can see that every time life threw me a curve ball, I always seemed to end up being in the right place, at the right time and meeting the right people. I was always guided to the place where I needed to be for the next part of my life journey.

After we had been sitting in circle for a while the universe decided to move us on a bit and it mixed things up for us both. June embarked upon a rather hot and steamy affair and fell in love. All her spare time and energy was spent with her new man and I saw less and less of her. I was delighted for her, she was so happy, but I missed her and our time in the Church became less.

Then my life took a big knock when my marriage collapsed and my my husband left. I was left alone in the house with a small child to support. To top that I was to be made redundant as the company I worked for was about to relocate to another part of the country. I had no time or energy left to give to the spiritual me and so that part of my life was well and truly put on hold.

I already knew Pat and Geoff, in fact, the four of us had been friends for years and Pat worked for the same company. It's when the chips are down that you really do find out who your friends are and Pat came up trumps. She had already decided that she was going to relocate with the company and one day she floated the idea that maybe I would like to consider it too. We could pool our resources and all start a new life in a different part of the country, and provide a better future for Jordan. I mulled it all over, it was a big step but I had this gut feeling that it was the right thing to do. I didn't really have anything to lose so I made my decision and I moved. We bought a house, I got a job and life was good.

- CHANGES -

Then I met Gill. Little did I know at that point what a major role she would have in my life.

Back then my ears used to constantly block and I would always have them syringed. One particular time, a colleague suggested I had them candled instead as it was much gentler on the ear. I had never heard of Hopi Ear Candling before and no idea where I would get it done, but it appealed to me so I Googled for therapists in my area and up popped Gill's name and contact details. Now I didn't know her from Adam, but she was only in the next village so I reasoned that she was as good as anyone else and I booked an appointment. Little did I know how significant that appointment would be and Gill told me much later that she had no idea how I found her as she never advertised on the internet.

As soon as I walked into Gill's therapy room I had the

overwhelming feeling that I already knew her and I also knew that meeting her would turn out to be more significant than I first thought. Over the next few years, my ears continued to block and I always went back to Gill. And then the cancer struck and life went on hold for a while.

During the years following cancer, there were some good times and some not so good times, but that's life, isn't it? I think we all experience both in our lifetime but it's how we deal with the bad times that can either make us or break us.

I had been cancer free for several years when life was to change again. My boss decided to relocate to another part of the country and although he asked if I would continue working with him, I didn't want to relocate, and neither did I want to commute. That was hard for me as I had been in the job for 20-odd years and I loved it. But then the opportunity of taking voluntary redundancy cropped up and so, not looking a gift horse in the mouth, I grabbed it. I found another job which I enjoyed and which I figured would take me to retirement, but it was not my passion.

As it turned out, my passion was not that far away although I didn't know it at the time.

- A NEW DIRECTION -

I had a few days off work and one morning I was ironing and watching a bit of day-time TV. Escape to the Country was on and the couple wanted a large house in the country with an annex so the woman could start her own Reiki Practice. "You could do that," said Pat, who was watching the programme too. "What?" I asked. "Learn to do Reiki and start your own business." She planted the seed.

I mulled it over for a few days, the more I thought about it the better it seemed. I went to see Gill and asked if she could teach me. No, she couldn't but she gave me the details of someone who could. I went home and Googled and amazingly this woman was running a

Level 1 training course the following week and she had spaces available. I booked on the course.

I loved Reiki, it seemed to come naturally and I enjoyed giving sessions to others. Reiki is taught at over 3, sometimes 4, levels and I knew from the start that I would take them all. It took me a year but eventually, I received my Reiki Master Teacher Certificate. Not only could I give Reiki treatments, I could teach it too.

About a year or so after I qualified I received an e-mail whilst on holiday from a lady asking if I held a Reiki Share Group. I didn't but I knew that was to be my next step, so I promised to get back to her when I got home. Once home I thought about how I would make it work. It's not really a Reiki Share Group with just two people and then I wondered whether Gill would like to join. She did, and offered her treatment room to hold our sessions in. I contacted the lady, told her it was on and she asked if she could bring her sister-in-law. Perfect!

That Reiki Share Group grew in numbers and before long there were too many of us to fit in Gill's room, so we moved over to the local village hall. We met once a month and some months we had around 15-20 people join us. Gill and I got to thinking that if there was a need for this sort of holistic healing then maybe there was a need for more spiritual type events in our area. We arranged a few different things and they were all well attended. We decided to start our own business!

- THE BITH OF COMO -

We were both warned by different friends that going into business with someone you hardly knew was a bit risky, and to think long and hard before we made any commitment.

Neither of us needed to and in June 2012, our Como Centre was born. We both followed our intuition, instinctively knowing that this was right for us. No, we didn't know each other very well but we would have fun learning and, oh boy, we have had so much fun over the years. It turned out that Gill and I were very similar, not only did we both have an interest in all things mind, body and spirit, we also liked a lot of similar things, we both loved to laugh – a lot – and we both loved being with people and having a good time. We were to become best friends as well as business partners and I know that when the business ceases to be we will still have each other. She is there for me when I need her and I hope I'm there for her. My ears have not blocked again since.

We called the business Como as it's an amalgamation of both our surnames and some beautiful Japanese Gardens. We had a business launch and the lovely Dominic James, Reiki Master and Author, came along and gave the opening speech. This was a very exciting time but also a bit scary. We continued to use our local village hall but what we really wanted was a place of our own, where we could leave all our stuff and not have to clear away all the time. But we didn't have any money so just held the thought that one day it would happen.

It happened sooner than expected and in the November of that year we were guided to a space that was perfect for our needs and available to rent. We still had no money but Pat, the amazing and wonderful person that she is, offered to lend us our first 6-months' rent. We signed on the dotted line and moved in on the 1st January of the following year. We had our own premises! Oh, the joy of manifestation and the Law of Attraction.

We started small but then we both started to learn new things. I enrolled on a lot of training courses, including meditation teacher training, past life regression, spiritual development, counselling, coaching, colour therapy, sound therapy, Angelic Reiki, Bach Flower Remedies, and so the list goes on. We worked hard, but we had the best time ever. It was our policy that we would take personal training and then teach what we had learnt to others. There is absolutely no point in holding onto knowledge when it could be of benefit to people and, to our minds, the more people who learned these modalities the more the world would ultimately benefit.

It was during this time that I learnt the many skills and modalities that I would use personally when life got a bit tough, and this steep learning curve was worth every effort, time, and money.

Gill and I had so much fun running our Centre. We offered training in wide range of mind, body, and spirit practices plus some healing sessions with Sound, Singing Bowls, and Gong Baths. We also held a few just for fun events with Psychic Cafes and Evenings of Mediumship, but everything we did was within the mind, body, and spirit remit. We met some weird and wonderful people along the way and some truly inspirational ones too.

- BREAST CANCER SUPPORT GROUP -

A few years later, another opportunity arose in the strangest of ways. I received an e-mail from a woman in Panama asking if I would take her through her Level 1 Reiki training. I thought it strange that she chose me when there must have been hundreds of Reiki Masters between Panama and here, but I've learnt that the Universe moves in mysterious ways. Lizzie came on that first morning of training and I liked her immediately. She was British and a medical doctor giving aid to those in need in the poorer communities of Panama. During our lunch break, we started chatting and she told me of her aunt who was going through breast cancer. I told her that I had been through it too and that dealing with the emotional issues was really hard. I also told her that I believed that every experience was a lesson for us to learn from but that I still had no idea what the breast cancer had taught me.

"Oh, that's easy," she said, "you have to help others to deal with those same experiences that you struggled to deal with".

Really? Was it that simple? We chatted for quite a while and she offered to give me all the help and support she could from a medical position. She also pointed out that we had a wonderful space at Como so wouldn't have to find anywhere to hold meetings. She was right, we had been guided to our centre and it would be the most perfect place in which to help people. I went home and thought about it, told Pat and Gill, and they both agreed and supported the idea. I wrote to my own medical team at the hospital and they supported the idea too. I also phoned other support groups to see how they started and how they ran their group. Everyone was positive and encouraging.

We worked on the details. We would meet on a weekly basis with Pat coming and helping, we would provide tea, coffee, and biscuits, offer Reiki and other holistic therapies, and possibly add a few talks every now and then. We wanted it to be a free service to all who came. We were lucky to get a local man on board who does lots of fund-raising events for good causes and met a local paramedic who was running in the next London Marathon and wanted to raise funds for a local cause.

We planned to launch the Group after I returned from holiday in October, which was so appropriate as it was also Breast Cancer Awareness Month.

During that October holiday, we spent our last week in Fort Lauderdale, Florida. One morning, walking through the hotel lobby to breakfast I spotted a poster for a Full Moon Party on the Friday evening. It piqued my interest so I asked the lady on the desk about it. She told me they held the event once a month and she gave Tarot Readings. She also told me that as it was October she would be donating her takings to a Breast Cancer charity.

I had been working with Tarot and Oracle cards for a very long time, in fact, I got my first Tarot deck when I was in my late teens. I used them mainly for myself and was not really interested in becoming a reader, but I could be persuaded from time to time to read for others. I had taken a training course and we taught Tarot at Como.

Now Pat, who's mouth sometimes engages before her brain, told this woman that I read Tarot too and she immediately invited me to join her on the Friday evening, giving readings. Whoa, hang on a minute, I was on holiday and I didn't have my cards with me. She proceeded to tell me where to find the nearest bookstore and she knew they sold cards there.

Oh, bloody hell, this was all shaping up to be an opportunity that I couldn't really ignore. I agreed to join her provided I could get the deck of cards that I wanted and that any money I made I could keep for my own Breast Cancer Group at home. She agreed and off I went to the bookstore. One of the assistants pointed me to the spiritual area and there on the shelf at eye-level was the exact deck I wanted and it had been placed with the front facing out rather than sideways like all the other decks!

I did the Full Moon Party and raised a substantial amount of money for our Breast Cancer Group. Thank you, Universe.

Como and the Breast Cancer Support Group ran for many years and it was only when Coronavirus hit in 2020 that we had to change the way we worked. Sadly, we had to close our Centre and the Support Group as we could no longer meet in groups, which meant that we couldn't earn money to pay the rent and our other expenses. I was devastated, but I realised that nothing stays the same forever and there was probably something else that I needed to do.

Little did I know that cancer would strike again a few months after that and my life would change once again.

- ANGELS -

I don't think I've told you yet about the Angels, have I? I've not always believed in Angels, I used to think they were just nice little things you put on top of the Christmas tree. My own Reiki Master used to talk about Angels constantly and I used to think she'd lost the plot. Then one day, I was home alone and for some reason reading a book about Angels. One chapter explained that it was possible to contact your own personal Guardian Angel and even told you how to do it. So, I did it, and I can remember thinking something along the lines of "ok Angel, if you're there what's your name?" The first thing that came into my head was Peachy.

"Peachy," I thought, "that's a bloody stupid name for an Angel," and I didn't think any more about it. When I went to bed that night I went into the bathroom and there on the floor was a little white feather. Now the window was closed, so there was no way that feather could have blown in, but there it was in the middle of the bathroom floor. Oh, my God, I thought, she's real! From that day on I've worked with Angels and I constantly talk to Peachy. I'm telling you this because I just want to show you how Angels work in many ways and if they can't get your attention one way they will try another.

Looking back, before I actually found the lump I had been aware of the odd twinge and itching in my breast. My right breast also seemed to be smaller than it was, but I just put that down to previous surgery and treatment. I do believe my angels had been trying to tell me that something was wrong, but I had ignored them. Maybe I had heard but I didn't want to go down that Breast Cancer route again so far easier to just think it was my imagination. So, my Angels took to Facebook!! Oh yes, can you believe that? I really do have state of the art Angels who use all this modern technology and social media. I saw a post from someone, I don't even know who, who shared a photo of her boobs and one looked exactly the same as mine and she described the same symptoms. I ignored it. A few days later that very same post was shared by a friend of mine. I couldn't ignore it any longer and as I felt around my boob I found the lump.

Rhonda, if you're reading this book it's you I have to thank. Oh, and I've never seen that post again.

- I DID IT MY WAY -

As I embarked on my second cancer journey I was determined that it would not be a repeat of the first time and that I would use all the things that I had learned over the years to help me to cope better. I had amassed a toolbox full of useful techniques that had the potential to help if I chose to use them. I won't tell you that it was all plain sailing because I certainly had my moments, but it was so different and much easier than the last time. What I was able to do now was recognise when things were going downhill and then do something about it.

I had learnt to trust and do what felt right for me and not do what others told me to do, which was right for me. Let me tell you that that was difficult because we have all grown up in a system that tells us what is good for us, what we should and shouldn't do, what we should and shouldn't believe, etc. I was told during my first cancer experience that chemotherapy was the way forward for me, but the very treatment that was supposed to save me turned out to be the very thing that was trying it hardest to kill me. Even our nearest and dearest, who all have our best interests at heart, do not always know what's best for us.

This time I did it my way.

- WHAT'S NEXT -

So where am I now on my spiritual journey? Good question. I have learned a lot, some of it I use, some I don't, but nothing is ever wasted. At this stage, I've come to understand that spirituality isn't a one size fits all. Some of what I listen to or read about doesn't sit well with me, and that's ok. Being spiritual or living a spiritual life doesn't mean you have to follow a certain path, live a certain lifestyle, practice certain rituals or blindly follow the teachings of others, neither does it make you better or worse than anyone else. Being spiritual for me means that if it feels right and resonates with my soul then I accept it, if it doesn't then I don't. I've also come to understand that spirituality is simple, it's only our humanness that makes it seem more complicated. I understand that energy, vibration and frequency are key and if I have to do another tour of duty on this earth then I think I would like to study quantum physics.

I've come to understand that love is everything, and I try to show my love to others in acts of kindness, empathy, compassion and just being there when needed, holding the space without judgement.

I've often been asked over the years whether I believe in God. I've been called the daughter of the devil when I've said I'm spiritual rather than religious. Let me tell you though that although I do not follow any organised religion, I do believe that there is a greater power out there and whatever we call that power, be it Source, Energy, God, Allah, etc, it's the ultimate source from which we all come and it is pure love and compassion. So yes, I believe in God but I know him by a different name.

I don't know where I'm headed next on my spiritual path but then I don't think any of us really do. I am happy to float around in the infinite field of all possibilities and see what turns up. For now, I'm living in the moment and enjoying my new-found love of writing – who knew that I would ever write a book.

MY SURVIVAL GUIDE

I'm not going to tell you what to do to help you get through your crisis, I can only tell you what I did. My story is about breast cancer, but your story could be something completely different. What I want you to know is that there are techniques available to you that, although won't necessarily take the problems away, can make dealing with them a whole lot easier. I know these techniques work, they have worked for others and they certainly worked for me. I got through my second cancer journey much easier and although I still went through my moments of falling into a dark place, they were short lived.

So, here's what I did for my second cancer journey, but you may be facing something completely different and so you will need to adapt it to suit your own personal needs and situation or even find your own techniques. I've given you just a brief overview of each therapy, if one of them sings to you then I would encourage you to find out more about it or find a therapist who can help you through the process.

- SELF-HEALING -

My first thoughts on learning that cancer had reared its ugly head again was that I needed to contain the little bastard that had taken up residence in my right breast. Time to call in the troops.

Although I am a Reiki Practitioner, I do both Usui and Angelic, I don't believe that you necessarily have to run out and take a training course in Reiki or any other healing modality. All you need is the intention and desire to heal. Visualisation or the ability to imagine and 'see' is also beneficial.

Your thoughts are energy vibrations and what you constantly think about is drawn towards you. That's why we're constantly being told to think positively. But that's easier said than done when you're going through a life crisis and, to be honest, can be totally irritating when people keep telling you to be positive. It's ok not to be positive all the time, it's ok to go to some dark and dismal places, that's all normal and we do have to deal with our emotions rather than keep suppressing them. But you don't want those dark places to consume you and sap all your energy. Neither do you want to turn into a permanently miserable sod.

Spend some time every day thinking about the outcome you want. That's where you place your attention. Then, think about the way in which you might achieve this outcome, and then visualise it happening. It doesn't have to take all day, start slowly and build up to a chunk of time that you are comfortable with.

In my case, I needed to first contain the tumour and so I visualised my troops marching up through my body to surround and contain the little bugger. After surgery and after the tumour gone, my intent was to destroy any rogue cancer cells that may have remained and to heal my body. My troops turned into super troopers destroying all bad cells and leaving behind a fresh supply of stem cells. I visualised myself as completely healed and happy.

Let me tell you how I visualise my Super Troopers. They look like Storm Troopers from the Star Wars movie, but that's where any similarities end. My Super Troopers are happy beings and they only want to help. When they march into my body they come dancing and singing Abba's Super Trouper, they're really rocking it to the music. I still continue to do self-healing for about 15-minutes every morning before I get out of bed. There's always something that could do with a bit of a boost.

As you've read in a previous chapter, I was greatly influenced by the work of Bruce Lipton, Gregg Braden, and Joe Dispenza – my three wise men! Just to give a little background on these guys, Bruce Lipton was a cell biologist whose research changed dramatically as he came to understand the importance of energy and how we can actually influence and change our own genes and cells. Gregg Braden, also a scientist, has worked in corporate business and now bridges science and spirituality in the real world. Joe Dispenza is a doctor and scientist and is driven by the conviction that each of us have unlimited abilities and the potential for greatness. You can learn more about these guys on their individual websites.

After reading their books and especially Joe's The Placebo Effect I started to work on some of my beliefs that were stored deep within my subconscious, and that were not serving my best interests. In fact, those deeply ingrained beliefs that I started to pick up from my family, friends and society from birth, actually held me back. I started doing the meditation that goes with the book and that certainly helped me to focus and start the change process. I would say, however, that it's one thing to change a belief or two, but it's a different matter knowing what beliefs you want to change. In my case I wanted to change the belief that I was limited in some way, that I would never achieve what others could achieve, that I was not quite good enough. This was a deep-rooted belief that I had carried from childhood and it really did need changing as it was holding me back.

It's taken a few months but I'm getting there. Now, instead of thinking 'I couldn't do that' my thoughts are now along the lines of 'yeah, let's give it a go'.

- CALLING BACK YOUR POWER -

My second tool was to call back my power. You already know that I decided from the beginning that I wasn't having chemotherapy again and I voiced that decision to everyone and at every opportunity along the way. That's me taking back my power, that's making my own decisions about how this whole cancer crap was going to play out. I was determined that I wasn't going to be strapped into that damned rollercoaster again with no way of getting off until it stopped. This was my body, my cancer, my life, and my bloody decisions!

Let's talk a little bit about our power and what it is. Our power is a vital part of our being. It has been a part of us since we were born. Our power is our essence, so to speak, it's the part of us that gives us that spark of energy and drive to "go for it". Gradually, as we get older, this power evolves into control. And as we move through our lives, we can either keep our control and watch it grow or we can give it away entirely. As crazy as it seems, it is not uncommon to give away our own power.

- We give away power when someone or something tries to get the better of us, or we've allowed someone or something to have a hold over us in a way that's stopped us from going for a dream, vision, or goal.
- We give away power when we allow someone to treat us, or someone close to us, in a bad or negative way.
- We give our power away when we say "yes" when we really want to say "no". We feel we don't have a choice because we need the job, because it's our family, because we don't want to rock the boat, and so on.
- We give away our power when we try too hard to please people, because we want to see others happy. But, in reality, it is not our job to make others happy, that's their job.
- We give away power over intense or traumatic situations that we can't let go of and keep replaying in our heads.
- We give away power when we blame others for our trials and tribulations. When we feel we have no control over our lives or a certain situation, we give away power.

- We give away power when we rely on someone or something else for our happiness. One of the main factors of unhappiness is the feeling that it is somewhere outside of us and that we have no control over whether we are happy or not. Our own state of happiness is closely linked to the amount of power that we have given away.

Constantly giving away our power can wreak havoc with our self-esteem and self-confidence.

We need to start to look at where we are giving away our power. Once we have identified those people or situations who take power from us, we can put a stop to it and start to regain control over our lives which, in turn, restores our self-esteem and brings us back to our natural state of happy and confident individuals.

So, how do we get our power back? First of all, you need to admit you've lost control and decide that you want it back. In my case, I knew I'd lost control during my first cancer experience as I went along with everything that someone said was in my best interests. I was determined I wasn't going to lose it during the second experience. I needed to find the right balance between what I wanted to happen and what I needed to happen to save my life. I knew that medicine and therapies had changed a lot in the 14-years between the two diagnoses, so I had to be sure that the decisions I made were in my best interests.

I spent some time thinking about me and how I saw myself. How you see yourself is how the world sees you. So, was I a little weak, easily open to suggestion and follow blindly, or was I strong willed and determined? I thought I was fairly strong, but then that could be how I wanted to be seen, so I got a second opinion from Pat who confirmed I was strong and determined and often too determined for my own good! That was good because it reaffirmed my belief in my own powers and abilities which equates to self-empowerment, and I needed to be empowered if I wasn't going to be swayed into having something that I didn't want.

If ever there was a time to be the writer, director and star of a chapter in my life story, it was then. This was never a love story but I knew that I wanted the happy ever after ending so I envisaged the whole thing from start to finish. I had no control over the cancer being there, but I did have control over my attitude to it and getting rid of it. The hero in my story was my gorgeous surgeon who not only did a great job in surgery but he really heard what I was saying. The baddie, if you like, was the faffing doctor who didn't really listen at all. I had a whole host of other stars who all played vital roles. I visualised all the scenes, the hospital appointments, the scans, the surgery, the follow-ups, and each one had the outcome I wanted. I knew that there would be a few dramatic scenes along the way, every movie has them, but even they ended positively. This was my life story and I was determined that this star was not going to have a tragic demise.

By taking back your power, whether it be in your job, your home, your relationships, or a situation you find yourself in, you give yourself the power to make the choice, your own choice, unhindered and uninfluenced by anyone other than yourself.

Acknowledge that you are in charge. It is your life. Decide what you want to do and take responsibility for the path on your life journey.

- MEDITATION -

This is another daily practice that I find so very valuable. I trained, many years ago, as a meditation teacher and so I fully understand the benefits it brings. It calms the mind and body and gives you that respite you need. It has 101 other benefits, but I won't bore you with them here.

On a physical level, it reduces brain wave activity from the very active alpha/beta states, bringing them down to the theta state which is what we are aiming for in meditation. Many people think that to meditate is to clear the mind of all thought but that couldn't be further from the truth, in fact, it is impossible to stop the mind. What we want to do is to give it something else to focus on so that it's not full unpleasant thoughts and crap.

Now let's be honest here, meditation doesn't come easily to everyone. It's a practice. It took me years to get the hang of it and even now some days are good and some days not so good. It doesn't matter that I have rubbish days, what matters is that I keep up the practice.

There are many types of meditation, so please don't be put off by trying it once and not liking it, you simply have to find the one that suits you. In my own classes, I teach 10 different types and my students all differ in what they like, but they all find something that suits them. My own practice is a mixture of different types, depending on my needs of the day. But if you want something quick and easy that you can do anywhere, then just use your breath.

Simply bring your attention to your breath and just repeat in your mind: *"I am breathing in; I am breathing out"*. Match your breathing with those words. Your focus is entirely on your breath and your mind is fully occupied. You are in control. Don't worry if your mind wanders after a while, and it will, just bring it back to your breath. I am breathing in; I am breathing out. You can do this anywhere and I've used it many times during hospital visits whilst I'm anxiously sitting in the waiting area.

But if you have more time and can relax, then guided meditations are hard to beat. Have a look around YouTube, iTunes, Spotify, or whatever platform you use, all have a range of meditations to suit specific needs. Choose something healing or relaxing. One tip I would give is listen to the voice before you spend money on a download – some voices are irritating and if you're constantly thinking about how much that voice is getting on your nerves, then you won't achieve anything from the meditation.

-MINDFULNESS -

This is another form of meditation, but rather than calming the mind and taking it off to somewhere nice and relaxing, in mindfulness we bring our attention to the present moment and focus on what's happening around us and what we are doing. A lot of the time we work on autopilot and the mind is left to wander where it will. Most of those mind wanderings are focused either in the past, reliving bad memories or regrets about what we should or shouldn't have done or said, or it's wandering to the future and becoming filled with fear and anxiety about what might be. With mindfulness, you focus totally on what's happening now and notice every little thing about it.

For example, if you drive a car you do it automatically, you don't have to think about changing gear or where your feet are and on which pedal; driving a car is so deep in our subconscious that we don't have to think about it. Before you know where you are you've reached your destination and probably can't remember a thing about the journey, which left your mind free to think about all sorts of issues and get more stressed and anxious about everything.

With mindfulness, we give the mind something to focus on, so if it's a car journey notice what's around you, take notice of the scenery, the car in front, and pay attention to how you're actually driving your car. Likewise, if you're doing a mundane task like the dishes, pay attention to the water, the soap suds, notice how they feel, what they smell like, etc. Bring all your senses into play, sight, hearing, touch, smell, taste. You get the picture? This isn't easy and you do have to keep bringing the mind back to what you're doing in the present moment, but it is beneficial and becomes easier with practice.

I will admit that I don't find this easy but one way that I can become totally mindful is to immerse myself in my hobby. I crochet. Yes, the old woman in me is beginning to emerge but then I will admit that I'm no spring chicken anymore. When I pick up my hook I am totally absorbed in what I'm doing and the more intricate the pattern the better. But choose anything that you love to do that demands your attention and whenever you find your mind is off doing its own thing, or your Elsie Ego kicks in, go and spend some time with your hobby.

- JOURNALING -

I started to journal years ago and I really love it. It gives me the freedom to say it exactly how it is and how I feel, and it doesn't talk back! Journaling goes much deeper than keeping a diary that's filled with dates, times, and stuff that you need to do, or have done, or what the weather's like, or what you had for dinner, or how much weight you've lost or gained, and so on. Journaling can be one of the most life-changing habits that you will ever form.

Journaling is a great tool we can use to help with trauma, stress, anxiety, emotional issues, grief, addiction, relationship challenges, and so on. It's a place where we can be totally open and honest about our thoughts, feelings, and emotions. It helps to improve mood and memory, encourages us to take the next positive steps, and, in some situations, reduces symptoms of chronic diseases. There are many other reasons to keep a journal, but I just want to use it here as a therapeutic tool to help get us through difficult times.

You may feel that you already talk about your feelings to those closest to you, but you probably gloss over the depth of your emotions. During upsetting or harrowing times, our more painful thoughts and feelings associated with that experience are often suppressed, leaving us unable to fully process what took place and unable to move on and heal from the experience.

Journaling about thoughts, feelings, and emotions when you're going through a life crisis, dealing with issues, or just daily life, can be hugely beneficial to our mental health.

When we journal, we allow ourselves free and authentic expression which helps us to figure out why we feel this way and then helps us to move beyond those thoughts and feelings. The journal becomes a therapeutic tool which heals, empowers and nurtures personal growth and creative expression. Once we better understand why we're feeling the way we are we can then do something about it.

You don't need to be a good writer and you don't need to do it every day if you don't want to, but regular writing is good. What you do need is to be absolutely honest and authentic in what you write. If you feel like shit then say so. But it's not enough to just say 'I feel like shit', you have to follow that up with why, what or who trigged those feelings, what does feeling like shit make you want to do, how do you think you can change that feeling, and so on. There is no right or wrong way to journal, it's all about you and will be as unique as you are. Let it be as messy as you like because life is messy. Doodle on some pages, allow it to become tear-stained on others. Coffee rings are fine too. My own journals are a total mess but they have become my very dear friends.

The first sentence is often the hardest to write, but once the words start just keep writing – allow it to flow. If you're not sure what to write about then start by writing about what's upsetting you right now. Date every entry into your journal. You can then reflect on how far you have come, what you've learnt from some experiences, and what further work you need to do. Don't judge what you have written when you read it back, it's how you felt at the time. It's neither right or wrong, it simply is what it is.

I started a new journal on the day I found the lump and every day I wrote something about how I was feeling. It wasn't always pretty, or positive, but it was completely authentic to how I was feeling at the time. The pages became messy, some were tear stained, sometimes the pen went through the page when I was angry and writing hard, some days my writing was neat and nice, others not so. But I was getting all those emotions down on paper rather than pushing them down somewhere deep inside. The days went by and I continued to write. Then one day as I was reading it back I thought that if I felt like that during my experience of breast cancer then so must others. And that's when the idea came to turn my journal into a book.

So, treat yourself to a lovely new notebook and pen, find a safe and secure place to keep it, and start writing.

-GRATITUDE-

A long while ago I decided to adopt an Attitude of Gratitude to see if it really did make any difference like all the spiritual people were telling me. I kept a Gratitude Diary and every day I wrote a minimum of 3 things that I was grateful for that day. To be honest, at the beginning I struggled – can you believe that? I struggled to find 3 things that I was grateful for! And then I started to get the hang of it. It didn't have to be anything big or spectacular, it didn't have to be something new that had happened, it didn't have to be amazing or remarkable. What it had to be was personal and something that I was totally grateful for. Some days it was so simple – a glass of wine or a bar of chocolate. Other days were mega, like Jordan arriving back home safe and sound. There's nothing that makes me more grateful than going to bed at night knowing my child is safely sleeping in his own bed and under my roof.

Now I never had a particularly good track record with keeping a diary of any description and I wondered whether I would give up after a few months or, knowing me, a few days. So, I took to Facebook and every day I posted my 3 gratitudes. I wanted to continue into the next year but thought my friends and family were probably already sick of it, so I didn't subject them to more. But during the year that I did it, not only did it become a habit it also held me accountable and made me keep doing it.

According to psychologists, being grateful for what you have can boost happiness and your overall sense of wellbeing. When you start to recognise and acknowledge everything you are grateful for, you become much better at recognising the good in your life. When you are actively grateful, you start to make gratitude your default feeling. The Law of Attraction works on the principle that what you spend time thinking about is what you attract back to you. It therefore makes perfect sense to start thinking about all the good in your life, being grateful for it, and having more of the same coming back to you.

So how, you may ask, can you be grateful when life is throwing shit at you? Well, in any situation, however bad it can be, there is always something to be grateful for, however small that thing might be. It's not easy, I know, we have all experienced extremely tough times – sadly it's part of life – but we don't have to be defined by it. I wasn't grateful to have cancer again, but I am grateful that it's enabled me to write this book which will, hopefully, be of help to you.

My starting with a Gratitude Diary and then writing on Facebook formed the habit and although I no longer write my gratitudes down, I do list them in my mind every night and say thank you. I do believe that by doing that I can more readily see the good in every situation or person and am much happier than the miserable cow I could be.

- ORACLE CARDS -

Another of my first thing in the morning routines is to pick a card from a deck of Oracle Cards. I've been doing this for years and it really does help me to find my focus for the day. You already know that I've used Tarot cards for many years, but Oracle Cards differ in that there is no structure, can have any number of cards in a deck, and there is no common theme. However, they can be extremely accurate and useful.

Oracle cards have been used for many years as a divination tool and are a great asset in providing a little direction and clarity in life. There are so many different decks available and not all of them are resplendent with Angels or have a spiritual theme. It doesn't matter what deck you work with, but it should resonate with you in some way.

Oracle cards work on energy and vibration. Our vibrations change daily, hourly, even minute by minute depending on how we are feeling, what we're thinking about, and so on, so as we shuffle the cards those vibrations are transferred to the deck. The card we choose will be the exact one we need at that time. I should point out here that the card that comes up for us may not always be the card we want, but it's what we need to know. It's pointless to shove the card back and try for a better one – I've done that in the past and ended up with the exact same card three times in a row. You have to accept the message if you are to benefit from it.

Each deck comes with an instruction booklet. If you have never used cards before then do read through the booklet and then put it away or even throw it away. Take time to get to know your cards, look closely at the pictures, and not just rely on the words. The picture is telling you something, it has a message for you. Use your intuition and take notice of how you feel.

I have a lot of different decks and I use them all from time to time, but the one I'm drawn to the most is Angels and Ancestors by Kyle Gray. Not only are the cards beautiful, they really do resonate with me, and although I don't always like the card of the day I do accept the message it brings. The message stays with me and reminds me of where I need to change, or where I need to place my focus, or what I need to do. The message is guiding me but of course, I still have free will so I can choose to accept it or not. I always choose to accept because I have already asked for guidance as soon as I picked the deck up.

Decks of oracle cards are readily available in any good book shop or, of course, on Amazon.

- AFFIRMATIONS -

These are a great daily reminder of all sorts of positive things that give you a bit of a prod if you're feeling a bit stuck. If you use Facebook then you've probably seen hundreds of them pop up daily.

When you start to take notice of these daily affirmations and the positive messages they offer, then positivity starts to become your default setting. Of course, it doesn't mean that you won't get upset and irritated, and yes, you will have negative thoughts and feelings from time to time - that's human nature. But what you will find is that you can quickly return to your default setting of being a much more positive person.

There are some lovely affirmation calendars available, Louise Hay and Wayne Dyer being particular favourites of mine, but why not make your own? Simply write 365 positive statements on separate pieces of paper, secure them all in some way, and then turn to a new one each day.

Gill and I made one for one of our workshops and I still look at it now. In fact, today's affirmation is: "Today I accept that I am doing the best I can with the knowledge I have". That's totally relevant to me right now as I sit and write this book and am plagued by the frustrations and doubts that every writer must suffer. I remind myself that I am doing the best I can.

- EXERCISE -

I make sure that I take some regular daily exercise. This doesn't come easy to me. To be honest, I hate any form of physical exercise that I have to do on a regular basis. I find it boring and it takes up time that I would sooner spend doing something else. I also hate getting hot and sweaty and puffing and panting all over the place. I've tried all sorts of exercise over the years, I've joined gyms, keep fit classes, pilates classes and all ended fairly soon after starting. I've even tried jogging but it's not comfortable when your boobs are jogging independently of each other and to their own rhythm. I've tried playing team sports but I'm not in the least bit competitive so hated the pressure that was put upon us all to win and then looking at the sulky faces when we lost. The best of the bunch was yoga but I think that was only because we got to lie down and meditate at the end.

But I don't mind walking. In fact, I actually love it when the weather is good and the scenery is beautiful. I enjoy walking alone as it gives me the head space I need to think, plot, and plan what I'm going to do next. Equally, I like walking with someone else as we chat and laugh. At the moment, Pat and I go off walking for about an hour every day and cover about 2.5 miles.

I like being outside in the fresh air, I love hearing the birds sing, and I love being in nature. Nature heals. I love to feel the warmth of the sun on my skin. There are so many benefits to be gained from regular exercise, from keeping the body healthy to keeping weight under control. It releases the feel-good endorphins which helps to elevate mood and mental health.

A couple of years ago we decided to do a 5k walk to raise funds for our Breast Cancer Support Group and I can honestly say I've never had so much fun walking as I did on that day. We laughed from start to finish. There was about 30 of us, all wearing pink bras with pink balloons filled with helium tried to the straps. What a sight we must have made as we walked along the main roads into our town centre. We had music playing, we sang and clapped and danced, and we waved to anyone and everyone. We certainly stopped traffic that day.

So that's me in a nutshell, that's my daily routine. I urge you to find your own daily routine, things you're comfortable with, and perhaps even try some new things that will really work for you. One of the main things for me was the need to feel in control of my life, I needed to feel proactive in ensuring that I got the positive results I wanted.

I will be honest, it wasn't and isn't always easy. Some days I simply couldn't be arsed!

Be you, be true to yourself. It doesn't matter what others think, this is about you. It's your life and your issues to work through. But do you know what? You can do this, you really can. There will be days when you'll lie down and think you can't, but you can. You get up the next day and you try again. I've got every faith in you, you've got this.

Remember that nothing in life stays the same forever. Everything is in a state of constant flux, and whilst you might think now that this is never going to end, it will. This time next year everything will be different.

AND FINALLY...

So, there we are, that's my cancer story and how I dealt with it twice. It didn't seem quite so scary the second time, but maybe that's because I had already been through it once so knew roughly what to expect. My spirituality has served me well as not only did I have Angels and other fabulous beings on my side, I also had a whole host of techniques that I could use to help myself.

At this moment, I am cancer free. There are times when I look at my body in the mirror and feel a little sad, but then I pop Barbara in my bra and I begin to feel more like me. I am extremely grateful that the cancer has gone from my body. I am really happy. I am grateful that the experience has given me the opportunity to write this book. Never in a month of Sundays would I have imagined that I would become a writer, but as the idea floated by me one day I grabbed hold of it and here we are. I have enjoyed this experience, even though it's brought up memories that I'd sooner not think about. But then maybe that's exactly what I needed to heal.

I don't know whether the cancer will come back, I sincerely hope not. But if it should then I know I have the strength and the tools to deal with it, whatever the outcome might be. I'm certainly not going to spend my days worrying about it because I have a life to live and more books to write.

Thank you for reading my story, I am grateful to you all. I hope it's resonated with you in some way and I hope that it's been of some use.

I wish you well and I hope that whatever you're going through right now doesn't last too long.

With love, Elaine

www.ingramcontent.com/pod-product-compliance
Lightning Source LLC
Chambersburg PA
CBHW061952070426

42450CB00007BA/1252